BY DANA MUISE

www.walterfoster.com

ABOUT THIS BOOK

Is there anything cooler than space monsters? No way. And who doesn't love drawing action-packed combat? Put the two together and you've got **How to Draw Space Gladiators**. This book will teach you how to draw alien space warriors as they fight to the death in the notorious intergalactic gladiatior arena aptly named **Space Monster Battle Planet**. Some will win, most will lose, but YOU will draw the action!

SOME ADVICE ABOUT DRAWING FOR BEGINNERS

All art forms take practice. It doesn't matter if it's drawing, writing, dancing, or playing music, the only way an artist can grow creatively is through practice. When I was a kid I copied everything—from my sister's Archie comics to the Sunday funnies. One time I copied an entire issue of *The Incredible Hulk* comic from cover to cover, including the ads! As a beginner, I found the best way to learn how to draw like the pros was to mimic what they did. It was a great exercise. In time I developed my own drawing style, but much of what I learned stayed with me to this day. Feel free to practice copying any monster in this book; heck, even trace it if you want. The important thing is that you are drawing. Over time some of the things you imitate will stay with you and develop into your own style. Most artists carry around a small sketch book and draw anything they can whenever they get a chance. What a great idea! Pick up a pocket-sized sketch pad and try drawing one monster every day. I promise you'll love it! Enough blabber, let's draw some monsters!

ON THE EDGE OF TIME, IN SOME UNCHARTED SECTOR OF THE UNIVERSE SITS A DRY AND DISMAL PLANET. ITS HOSTILE WEATHER AND SUN-SCORCHED LANDSCAPE PROVIDE THE PERFECT BACKDROP FOR THE MOST FANTASTIC GLADIATOR GAMES OF ALL TIME...

WELCOME TO *SPACE MONSTER BATTLE PLANET!*
SPACE MONSTER BATTLE PLANET
HERE YOU WILL SEE THE MOST TERRIFYING GLADIATORS FIGHT TO THE DEATH UNTIL ONLY ONE IS LEFT STANDING TO CLAIM THE TITLE OF *MOST POWERFUL WARRIOR IN THE UNIVERSE!*

CHALLENGERS FROM EVERY GALAXY ARE TRAINED SINCE BIRTH FOR THIS SOLITARY BLOOD-SOAKED COMPETITION. SOME ARE INDEPENDENT, BUT MOST BELONG TO A PROFESSIONAL GLADIATOR TEAM.
TEAM OWNERS ARE OFTEN TYRANTS WHO DEMAND ALL THE GLORY WHILE THEIR GLADIATORS FIGHT AND DIE. TWO OF THE MORE FAMOUS RIVAL TEAMS ARE CLOSING IN ON THIS YEAR'S CHAMPIONSHIP.
TEAM ZORT
COME ON, YOU'VE BEAT BIGGER GUYS THAN THIS ONE!
ZORT ISN'T A BAD GUY, BUT HE DOESN'T HIDE THE FACT THAT HE'S IN IT FOR THE MONEY. THE CHAMPIONSHIP TITLE IS HIS TICKET TO FAME AND FORTUNE, WHATEVER THE PRICE!
TEAM PSYCHOZOID
IF YOU DON'T WIN THIS ROUND YOU'LL BE BACK SPLITTING ROCKS ON THE PRISON PLANET OF GULAG7, YOU PATHETIC IMBECILE.
TEAM PSYCHOZOID IS CONTROLLED BY ZORT'S ARCH NEMESIS: THE PSYCHOZOID, AN EVIL GENIUS BENT ON WORLD DOMINATION.
THE PSYCHOZOID PLANS ON USING THE WEALTH AND FAME FROM THE GLADIATOR CHAMPIONSHIP TO COMPLETE HIS EVIL PLANS. ZORT DOESN'T KNOW IT, BUT THE FATE OF THE UNIVERSE DEPENDS ON HIM.

RAED'AEUSNNTA'JHIY IEBHE AHEFVI!
YOU DIE FOR TEAM PSYCHOZOID NOW!
SLAM
YOUR MAJESTY, AS YOU CAN SEE MY WARRIORS HAVE ELIMINATED ALL OF ZORT'S GLADIATORS, WITH VERY LITTLE EFFORT I MIGHT ADD. THE CHAMPIONSHIP TITLE IS RIGHTFULLY MINE.
HMM, I WAS AFRAID OF THIS. PSY-CHOZOID, EVERYONE KNOWS YOU'RE GOING TO USE THIS PRIZE MONEY TO FINANCE SOME TERRORIST PLOT, BUT RULES ARE RULES.

I PROCLAIM TEAM PSYCHOZOID STANDS UNCHALLENGED AND THEREFORE WINS THE TITLE OF SPACE MONSTER BATTLE PLANET CHAMPION.
THAT IS... UNLESS ZORT HERE HAS ANOTHER CHALLENGER WE DON'T KNOW ABOUT...
...ZORT?
?
UHH... YES, OF COURSE I DO YOUR MAJESTY! I TOTALLY FORGOT ABOUT HIM! WON'T BE A MINUTE...
WHAT?
MUST FIND A GLADIATOR... MUST FIND A GLADIATOR...
NOBODY LEFT! WHAT AM I GONNA DO?
YOU THERE! LET'S GO, TIME FOR YOUR BIG MOMENT! COME ON, WAKE UP!

COME ON, WAKE UP I SAY!
CRASH!
HOW'S IT GOING IN THERE ZORT? WE'RE ALL WAITING....
UH... WE'LL BE RIGHT OUT! JUST GETTING HIM SUITED UP!
YOUR HIGHNESS, THIS IS AN OUTRAGE! I NEVER GET THESE KINDS OF BREAKS!
OH SHUT UP, PSYCHOZOID. YOU'LL GET WHAT'S COMING TO YOU. HONESTLY, I DON'T KNOW HOW YOU GOT THIS FAR.
OH MAN, WHAT AM I GONNA DO??
HEY YOU! YOU HAVE TO HELP ME. YOU NEED TO CREATE A WARRIOR STRONG ENOUGH TO DEFEAT THE EVIL PSYCHOZOID.
DON'T WORRY, YOU CAN DO IT! JUST FOLLOW MY DIRECTIONS—WE DON'T HAVE MUCH TIME!

Deke Drifter

DEKE DRIFTER COMES FROM A SMALL TOWN IN CENTRAL IOWA, OR MAYBE HE'S FROM SOUTHERN CALIFORNIA... IT DOESN'T MATTER. HE'S YOUNG AND INEXPERIENCED, BUT HE WILL LEARN WITH EACH BATTLE. DEKE WILL BE UP AGAINST THE BIGGEST AND STRONGEST OPPONENTS IMAGINABLE, SO GIVING HIM A PUMPED-UP BODY WOULD BE POINTLESS. WE'RE GOING TO CREATE A LEAN, SVELTE WARRIOR THAT RELIES ON HIS WITS AND AGILITY.

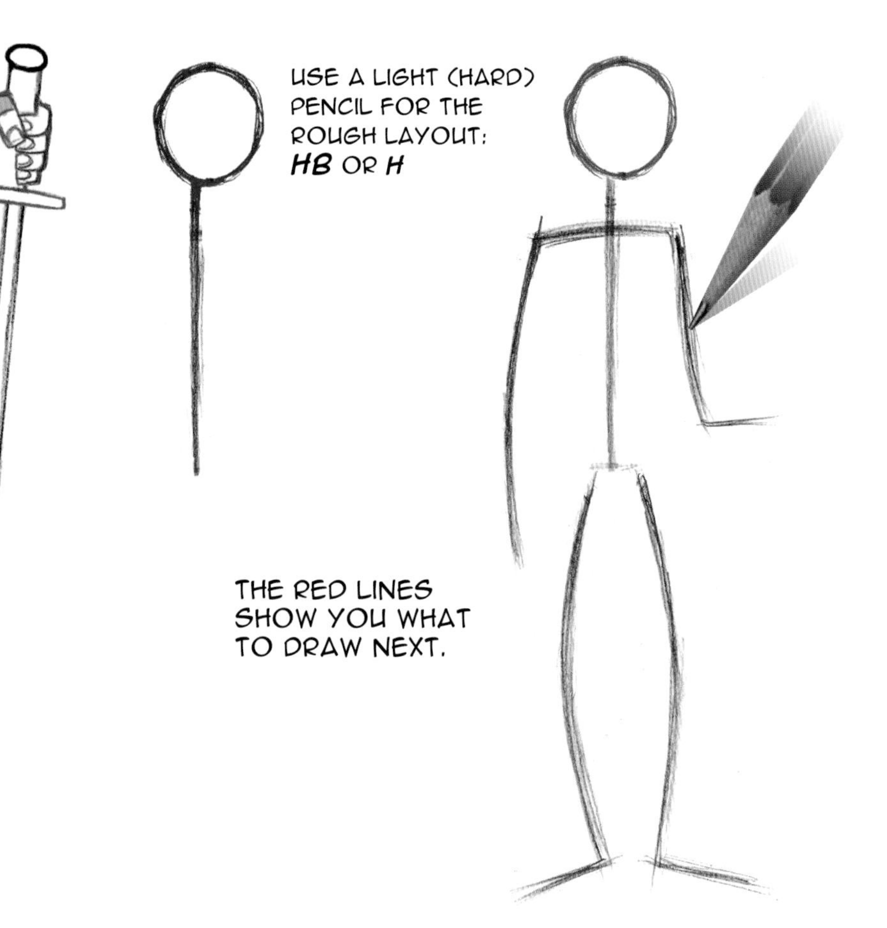

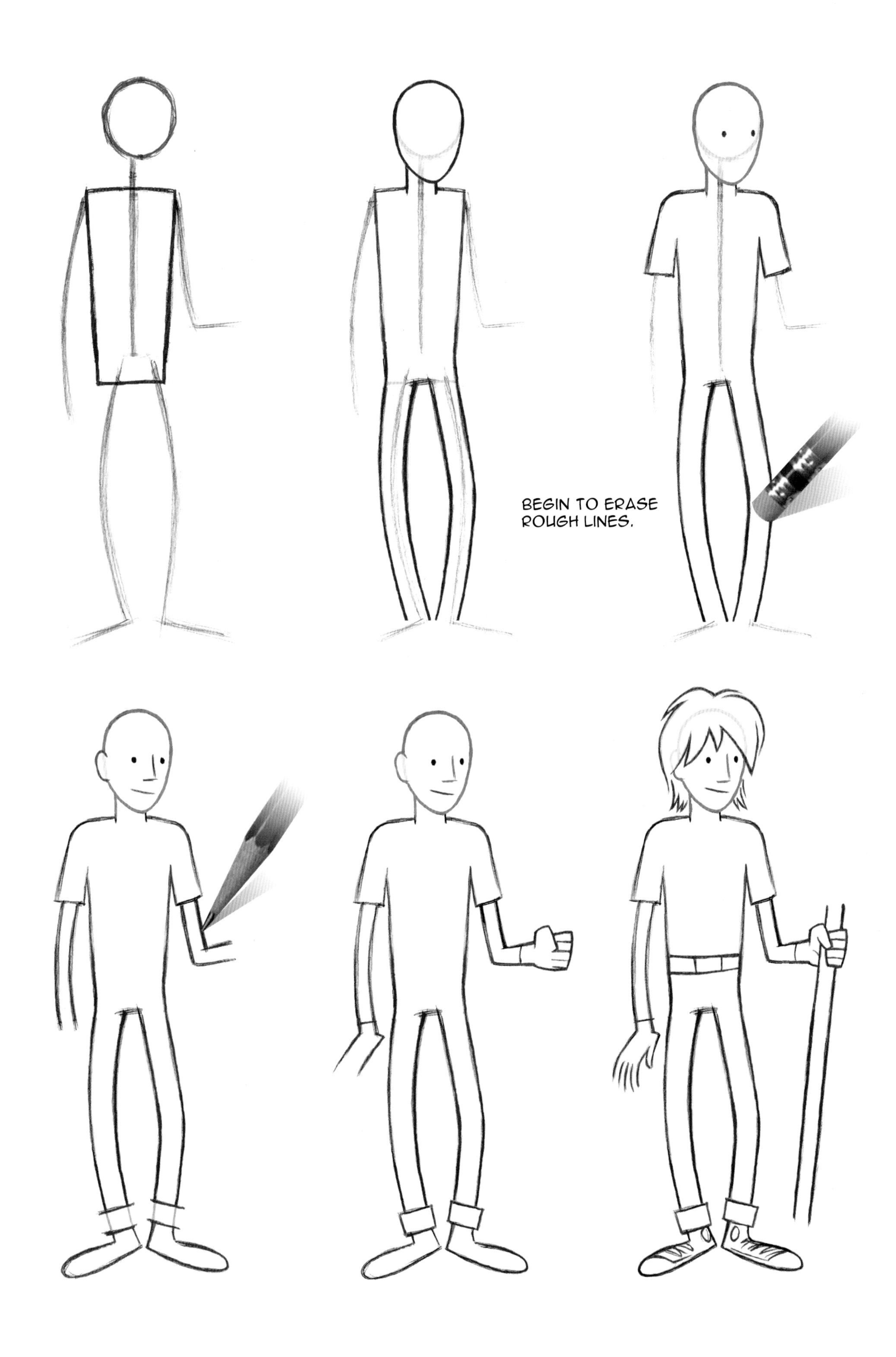
BEGIN TO ERASE
ROUGH LINES.

SEE, THAT WASN'T SO HARD! LET'S TRY ANOTHER ONE. THIS TIME GIVE DEKE AN ACTION POSE.

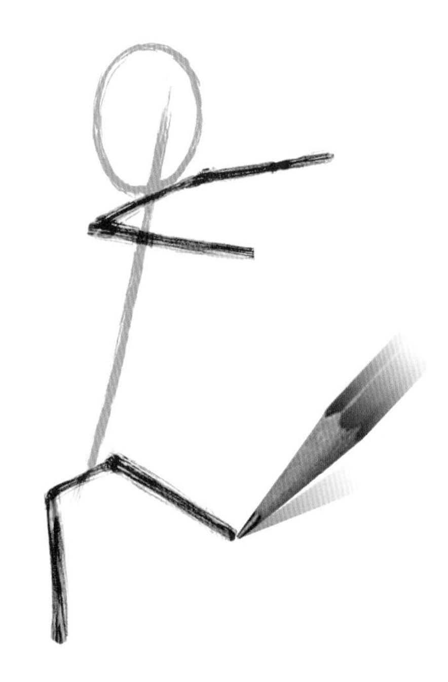

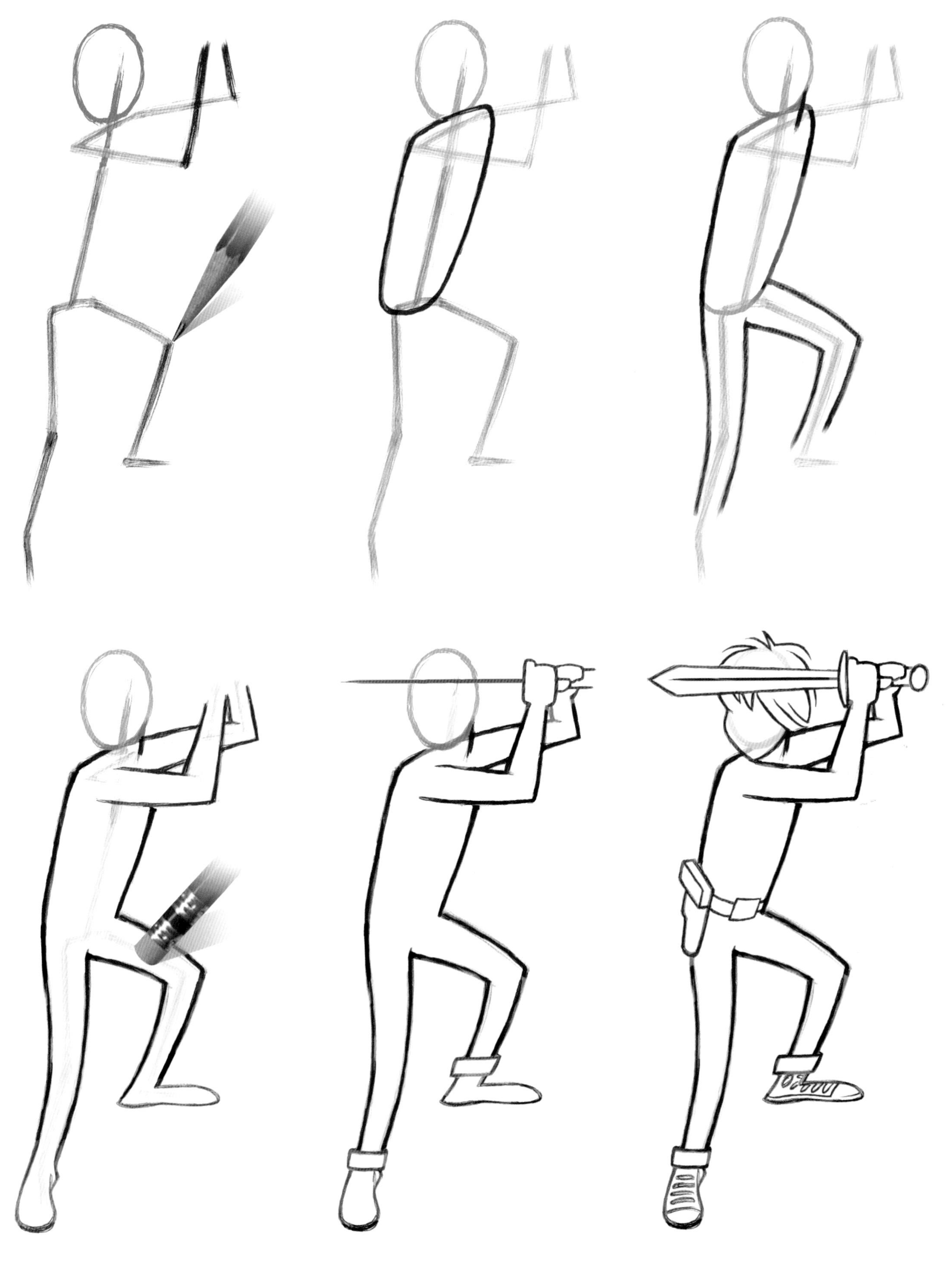

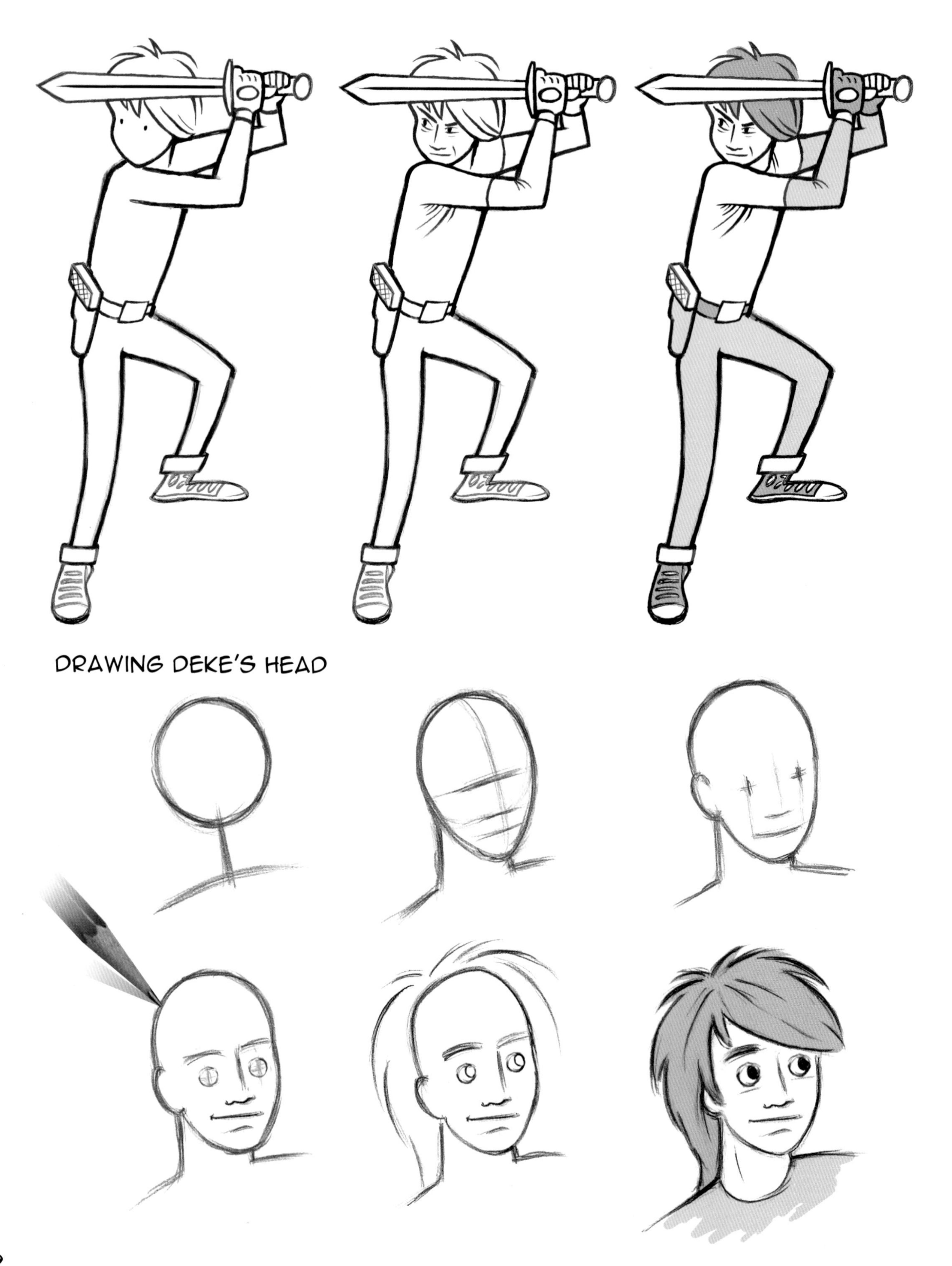
DRAWING DEKE'S HEAD

YOUR MAJESTY, WE'VE WAITED LONG ENOUGH! IT'S OBVIOUS HE HAS NO MORE GLADIATORS. I DEMAND THE CHAMPIONSHIP TITLE...
WAIT!
WAIT!
'SCUSE ME, PARDON ME...
HERE HE IS YOUR HIGHNESS.
ZORT, THIS SCRAWNY BIPED IS YOUR CHALLENGER?
WELL SURE! OKAY SO HE'S A HUMAN, BUT IT'S THE BEST I COULD DO GIVEN THE CIRCUMSTANCES.
DON'T BE FOOLED. HE'S LIKE A WILD ANIMAL IN THE BATTLE ARENA!
LET'S GET ON WITH THIS ALREADY, I'VE GOT A YOGA CLASS AT 4...
THORCLOPS, KILL HIM!
HOLD YOUR HORSES THERE PSYCHOZOID. I NEED TO SHOW THE FOLKS AT HOME HOW TO DRAW YOUR THOR-CLOPS THINGY, UGLY AS HE IS.

Thorclops

THIS CHALLENGER HAILS FROM THE ICY PLANET OF SVENTURIAN. THORCLOPS "THE DESTROYER" IS STRONG BUT EASILY OUT-MANEUVERED. HIS SINGLE EYE DOESN'T PROVIDE HIM WITH MUCH VISION, AND HE'S VULNERABLE IF BLINDED. STAY CLEAR OF HIS MIGHTY HAMMER: IT CAN ANNIHILATE AN OPPONENT WITH A SINGLE BLOW.

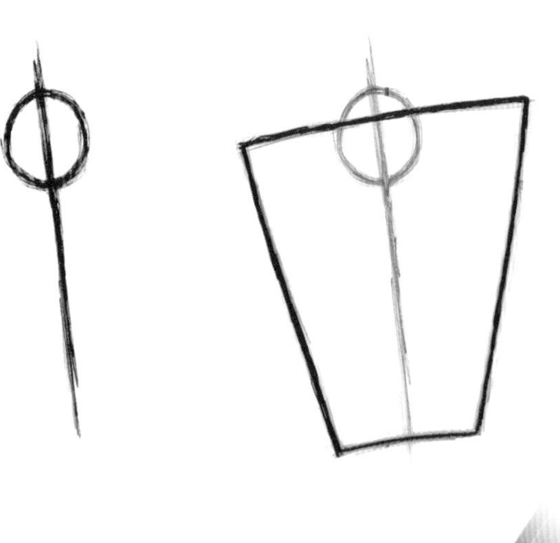

BEGIN TO ERASE ROUGH LINES.

ENOUGH OF THIS NONSENSE. LET'S HAVE THIS EARTHLING'S HEAD ON A STICK! I DON'T HAVE ALL DAY YOU KNOW.
OKAY, NOW IT'S ALL YOU DEKE. DON'T BE NERVOUS.
UH, 'SCUSE ME MR. SNORT...
THAT'S ZORT
OH SORRY, UH WHAT AM I DOING HERE ZORT?
NO TIME TO EXPLAIN, TAKE THIS BROADSWORD.
WHY DO I NEED THIS?
WHEN IT HAPPENS YOU'LL KNOW.
LADIES AND GENTLEMEN, INTRODUCING MY NEWEST GLADIATOR, ALL THE WAY FROM PLANET EARTH, LET'S GIVE IT UP FOR *DEKE DRIFTER!*
HEY I THINK THEY LIKE ME!
THAT'S GREAT. TRY AND STAY ALIVE WHILE I FIND ANOTHER GLADIATOR.
WHAT DO YOU MEAN STAY-
HEY, WHERE DID HE GO?
CLANG!

GAAA!!
SMASH
ZORT! HELP ME!!
BOO!
BOO
BOO!!
A HUMAN? WHAT WAS I THINKING?
HUP!

STAND AND FIGHT THORCLOPS YOU COWARD!
OH PEW! DON'T THEY HAVE DENTAL FLOSS ON YOUR PLANET?
THORCLOPS SQUASH YOU NOW!
EVEN THOUGH DEKE'S GETTING THRASHED HERE, YOU GOTTA LOVE THIS SHOT. LET'S DRAW IT!
MOMMY!

NOTES ABOUT FORESHORTENING

FORESHORTENING HAPPENS WHEN SOMETHING LONG IS POINTING STRAIGHT AT YOU AND THE LENGTH IS HIDDEN. IF YOU'RE DRAWING A LITTLE GUY WITH SHORT ARMS KEEP THE HAND SMALL.

BUT WITH A BIG GUY WITH LONG ARMS, MAKE THE HAND MUCH BIGGER. IT INCREASES THE FORESHORTENING EFFECT.

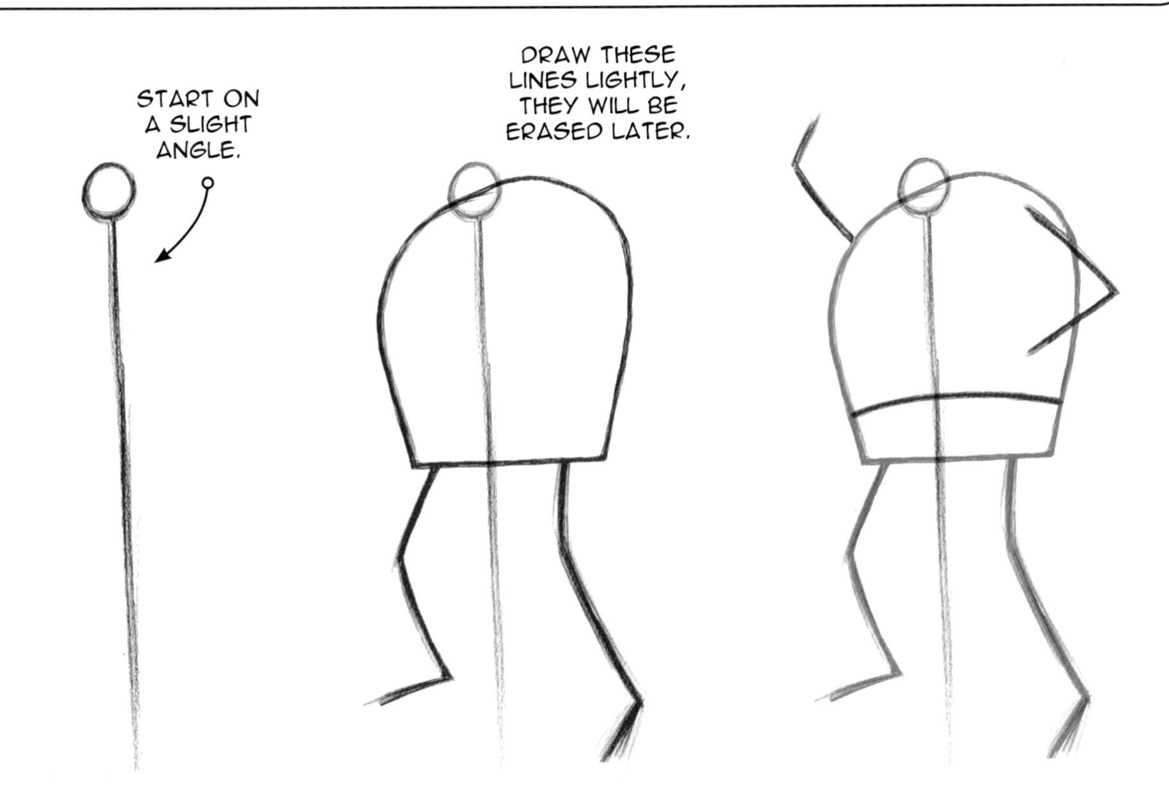

ERASE SOME OF
THE ORIGINAL
LINES.

LIGHTEN THE ORIGINAL OUTLINE OF HIS COAT WITH YOUR ERASER. ADD THE FUR; THEN ERASE THE LINE COMPLETELY.

THE MIGHTY THORCLOPS HAMMER, A MAGICAL WEAPON THAT IS SAID TO ALWAYS RETURN TO THE HAND AFTER IT HAD BEEN THROWN.

UH!
CLANG
HMPH! EARTH-MAN NOT SO LUCKY NEXT TIME!
DEKE! FOR CRYIN' OUT LOUD, YOUR GUN! USE YOUR GUN!
HUH? I DIDN'T EVEN KNOW I HAD A GUN.
EAT LEAD YOU ONE-EYED WASTE PRODUCT!
POW
POW
POW
POW
POW
STUPID HUMAN, NOT EVEN COME CLOSE TO HITTING THORCLOPS!
WHIZZZZ
ZING

BOINK!
OW!! WHY YOU LITTLE...
SO ZORT, ANY ADVICE ON HOW TO HANDLE THIS GUY?
WELL, HE'S ONLY GOT ONE EYE. THAT'S HIS WEAK SPOT! SEE IF YOU CAN BLIND HIM.
WAIT...
WAIT...
NOW!
MY EYE! AAARRRG!!
GOT 'EM!
GOOD, NOW PICK UP YOUR SWORD AND RUN HIM THROUGH!
THWAK!
PLING!

EARTHMAN FIGHTS LIKE LITTLE GIRL!
POW!
WATCH IT DEKE, HE'S COMING UP BEHIND...
WHAK!
...YOU!
GIVE UP NOW, AND THORCLOPS MAKES SURE YOUR DEATH IS QUICK.
OKAY, BUT THERE'S ONE THING I HAVE TO SAY...
YOUR SHOE LACE IS UNTIED.
REALLY?

YOU'RE EVEN DUMBER THAN YOU LOOK!
WOW! DEKE'S FIRST OFFEN-SIVE MOVE IS IMPRESSIVE! LET'S TAKE A MOMENT AND DRAW THIS ACTION SCENE!
SOUND EFFECTS DO MORE THAN DESCRIBE SOUNDS; THEY REPRESENT THE SOUND IN A VISUAL WAY. AND DON'T WORRY ABOUT GRAMMAR—SPELL IT JUST THE WAY IT SOUNDS!
BLAMMO!
BLAMMO!

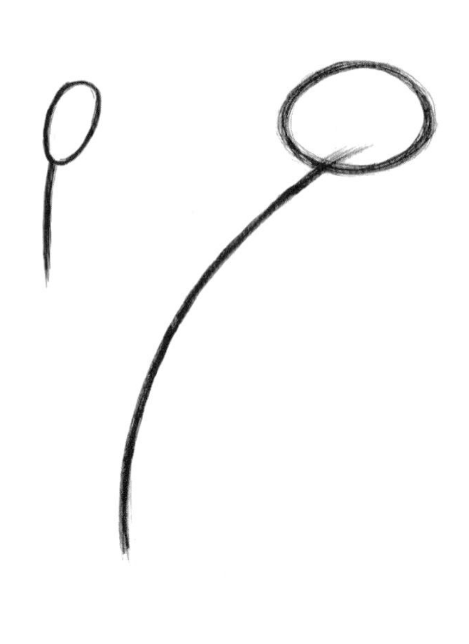

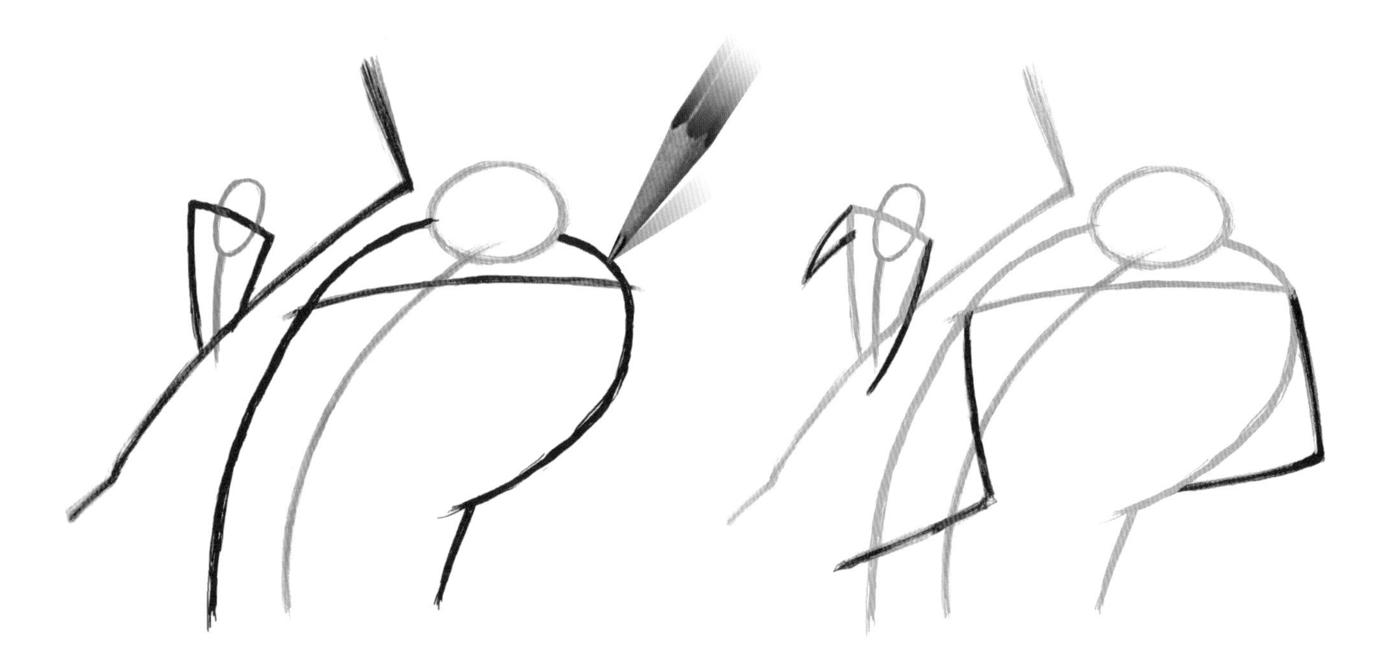

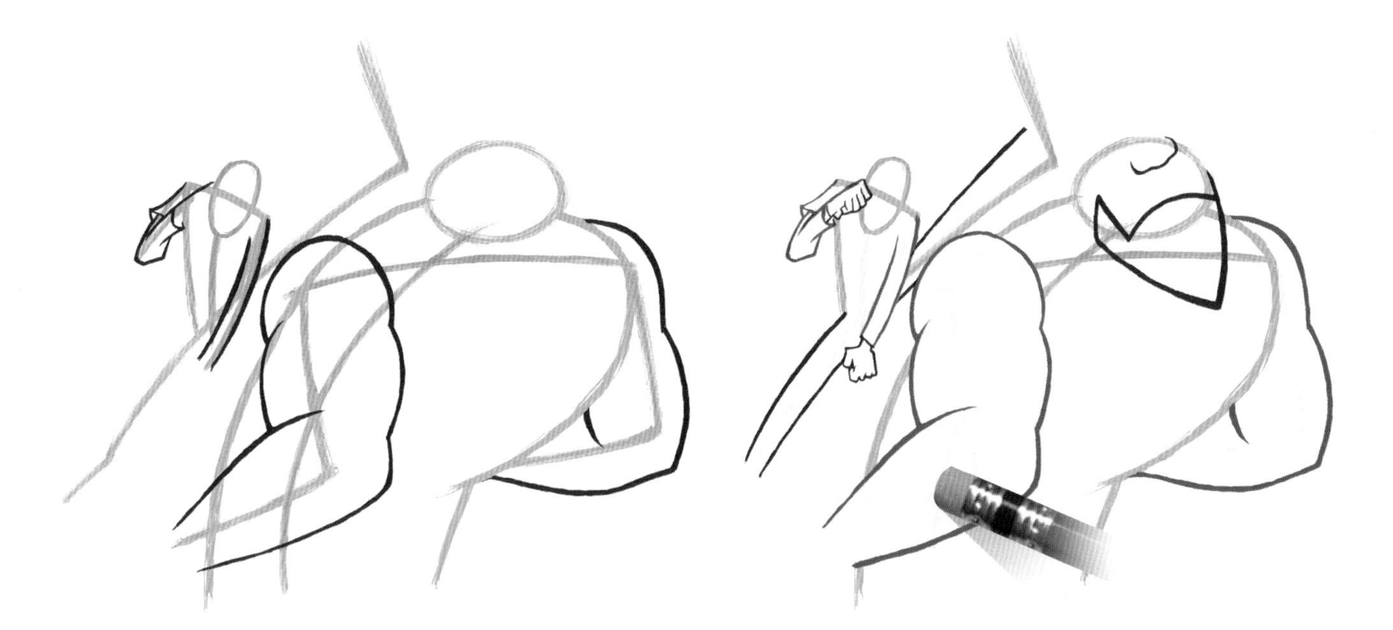

ERASE SOME OF
THE ORIGINAL LINES.

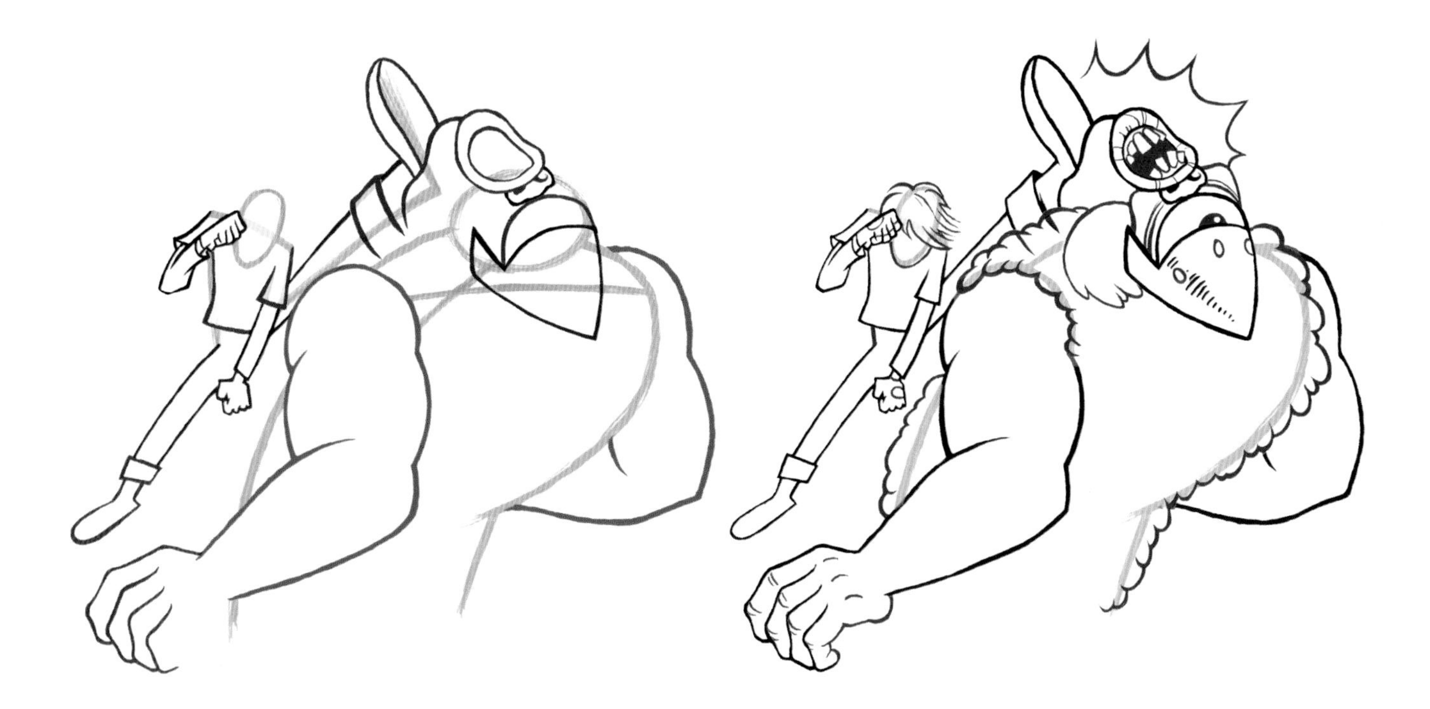

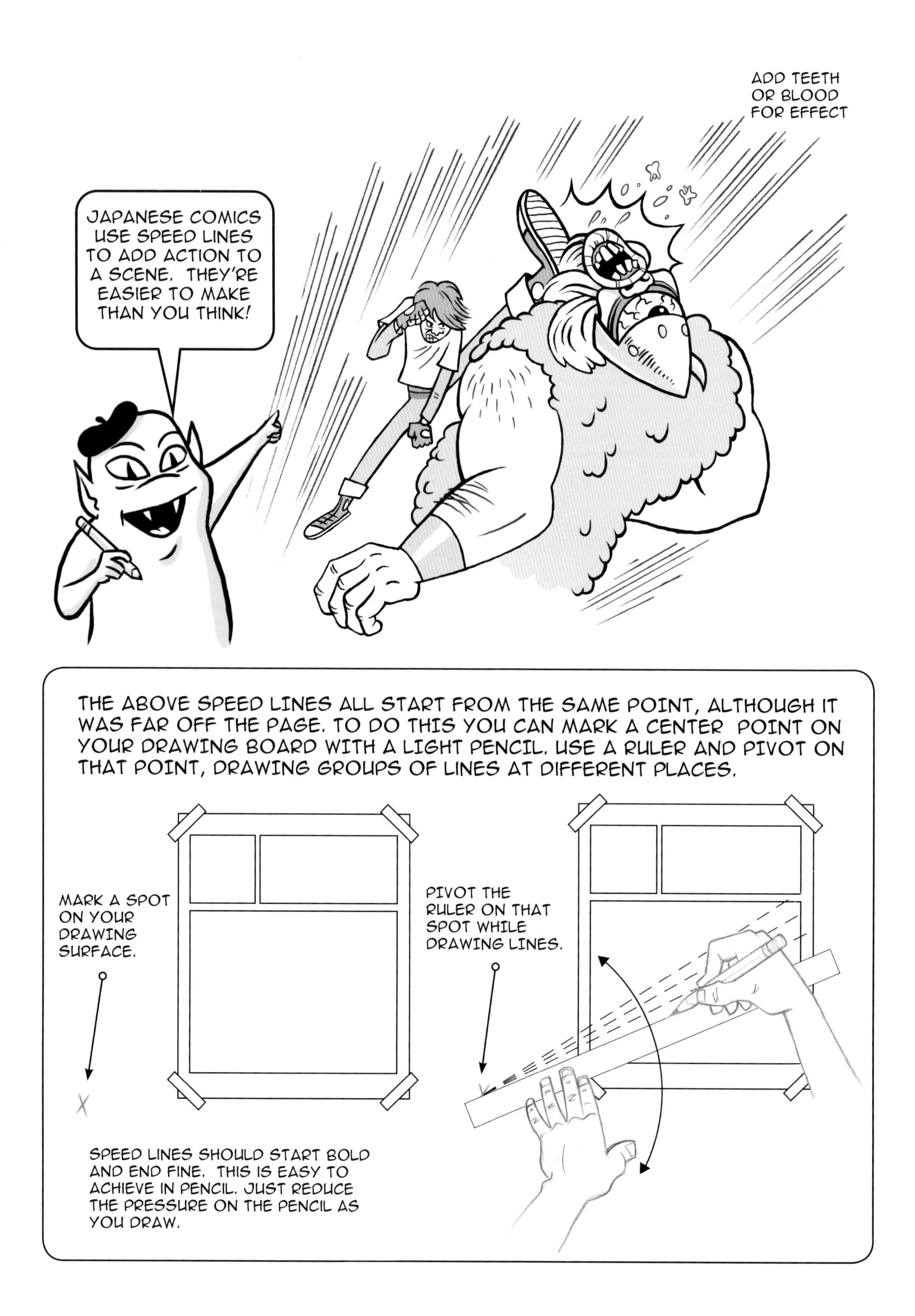
JAPANESE COMICS USE SPEED LINES TO ADD ACTION TO A SCENE. THEY'RE EASIER TO MAKE THAN YOU THINK!
ADD TEETH OR BLOOD FOR EFFECT
THE ABOVE SPEED LINES ALL START FROM THE SAME POINT, ALTHOUGH IT WAS FAR OFF THE PAGE. TO DO THIS YOU CAN MARK A CENTER POINT ON YOUR DRAWING BOARD WITH A LIGHT PENCIL. USE A RULER AND PIVOT ON THAT POINT, DRAWING GROUPS OF LINES AT DIFFERENT PLACES.
MARK A SPOT ON YOUR DRAWING SURFACE.
PIVOT THE RULER ON THAT SPOT WHILE DRAWING LINES.
SPEED LINES SHOULD START BOLD AND END FINE. THIS IS EASY TO ACHIEVE IN PENCIL. JUST REDUCE THE PRESSURE ON THE PENCIL AS YOU DRAW.

A LUCKY SHOT!
OH YEAH? WATCH THESE OTHER LUCKY SHOTS I TAUGHT HIM!
EARTH
PUNCH!!
THE "TOOTH EXTRACTOR"
THUD THUD THUD THUD!
THE IRON-FIST HEART MASSAGE...
AND THE CROWD GOES CRAZY!
AND, OF COURSE, THE THOUSAND-PALM PUMMEL, BREAKING EVERY BONE IN THE VICTIM'S BODY.

THORCLOPS... HAS... BEEN...
DEFEATED!
WE DID IT KID!
UH, WHAT DO YOU MEAN WE?
COME ON, WE'RE A TEAM.
WINNER!
SO, LISTEN ZORT, I WAS THINKING... SINCE I WON, DO YOU THINK I COULD... YOU KNOW, UM... GET THE HECK OUT OF HERE AND GO BACK TO EARTH?
THAT'S A GOOD IDEA! I DON'T SEE WHY NOT...
EXCUSE ME LADIES, I DON'T MEAN TO INTERRUPT, BUT I WOULD LIKE TO INTRODUCE YOU TO MY NEW FRIEND. HE'LL MAKE SURE YOU GET BACK TO EARTH ALL RIGHT...
IN A BODY BAG!
W-W-WHAT'S THAT THING?
HOLY SHNIRT! IT'S A SABER-TOOTHED SPACE DEVIL!
YOU KEEP HIM BUSY WHILE I TEACH A QUICK DRAWING CLASS!
WHAT?!?
ROOAR!

Saber-Toothed Space Devil

THIS CREATURE IS EVERY BIT AS TERRIFYING AS IT SOUNDS. HE COMES FROM THE DISTANT ANDROMEDA GALAXY AND STANDS A MASSIVE 25 FEET TALLER THAN HIS HUMAN OPPONENT. IF HIS RAZOR-SHARP FANGS DON'T TEAR YOU IN HALF, HIS GIANT CLUBBED TAIL WILL KNOCK YOU SENSELESS. HIS RAVENOUS APPETITE IS HIS ONLY WEAKNESS. TRY AND USE THAT TO YOUR ADVANTAGE.

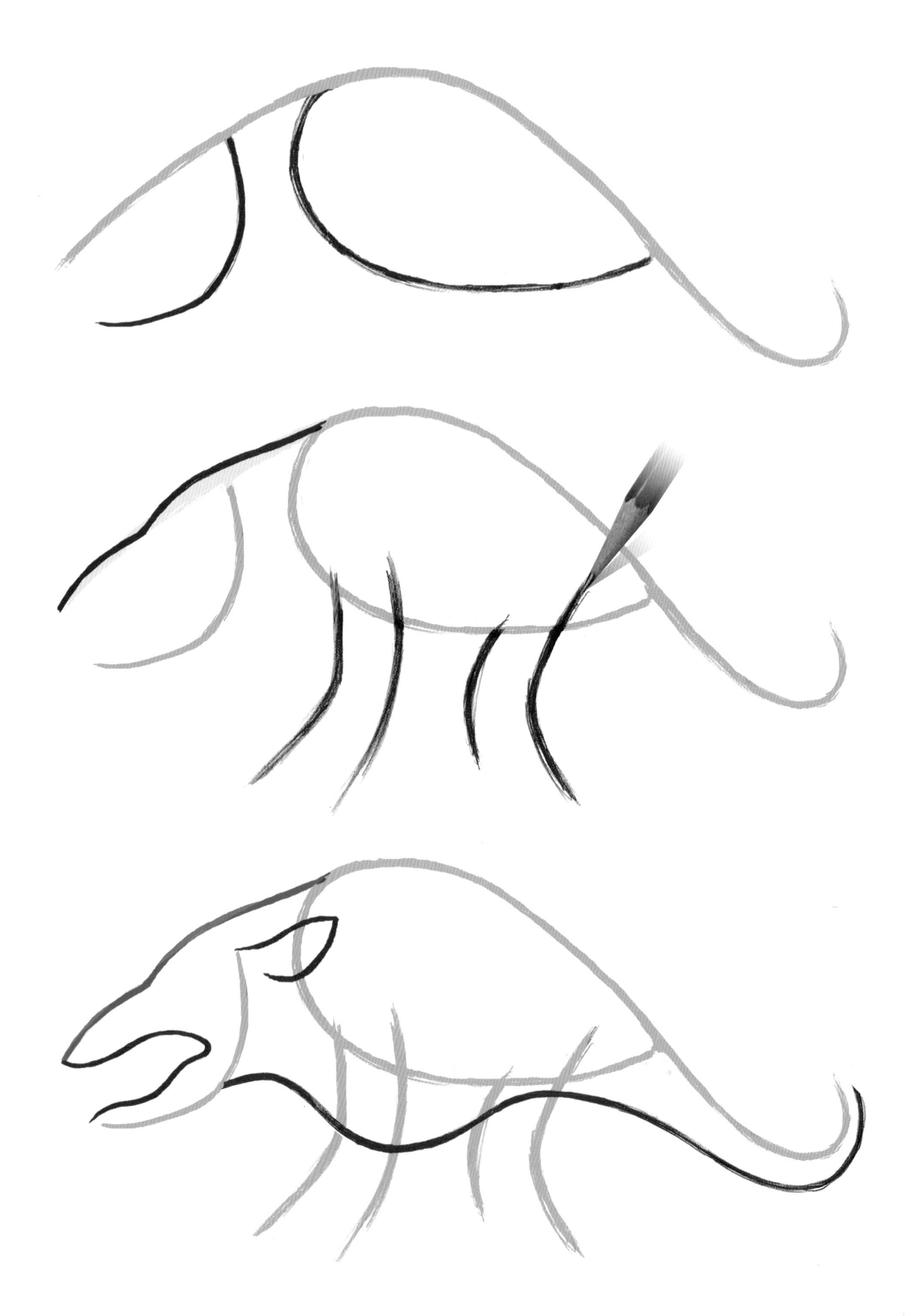

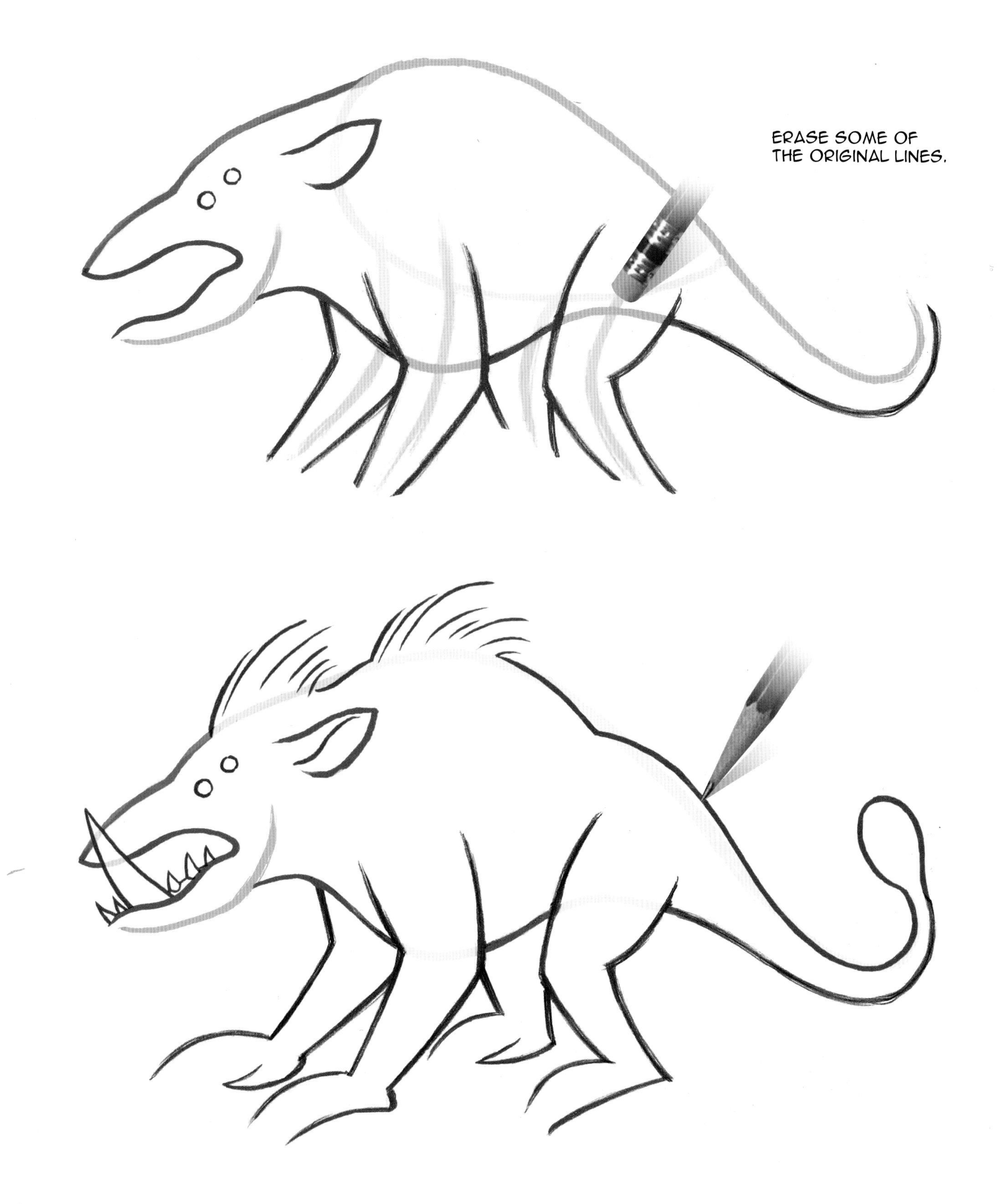
ERASE SOME OF
THE ORIGINAL LINES.

ZORT! DON'T LEAVE ME OUT HERE ALONE!
POW
A GRAND-SLAM! OUT OF THE PARK, LADIES AND GENTLEMEN!
NOT QUITE.
SPLAT!
drink ASTRO Cola
QUICK! GRAB YOUR PENCIL, AND LET'S DRAW BEFORE IT'S TOO LATE!

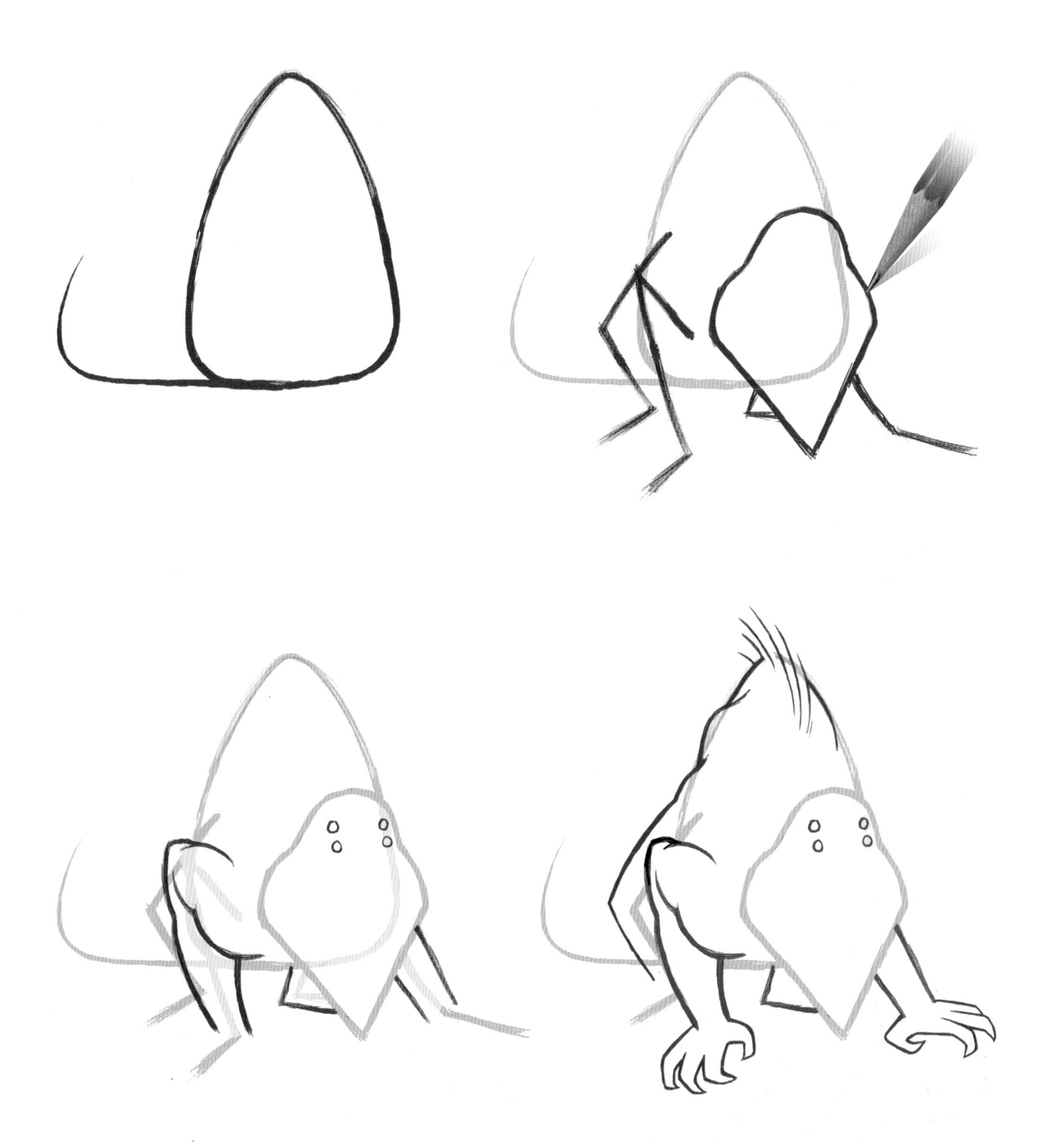

AS YOU ALREADY KNOW, DRAWING PENCILS COST MONEY. DON'T THROW THE LITTLE STUBS AWAY. INSTEAD, GET YOURSELF A PENCIL EXTENDER TO GET THE MOST OUT OF EVERY ONE OF THOSE SUCKERS!

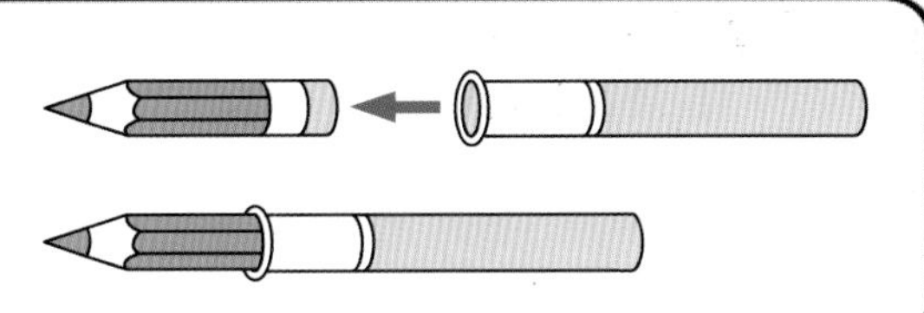

I CAN'T DIE NOW...THERE'S SO MANY THINGS I HAVEN'T DONE YET!
SO MANY PLACES I'VE NEVER BEEN...
SO MANY UGLY FACES I HAVE TO SMASH...
SUCH AS YOURS!
PUNCH
AWWW! LITTLE BABY GONNA CRY NOW?

ROAR!
OH BOY, NOW HE'S REALLY MAD. BUT IT'S A GOOD ACTION POSE.

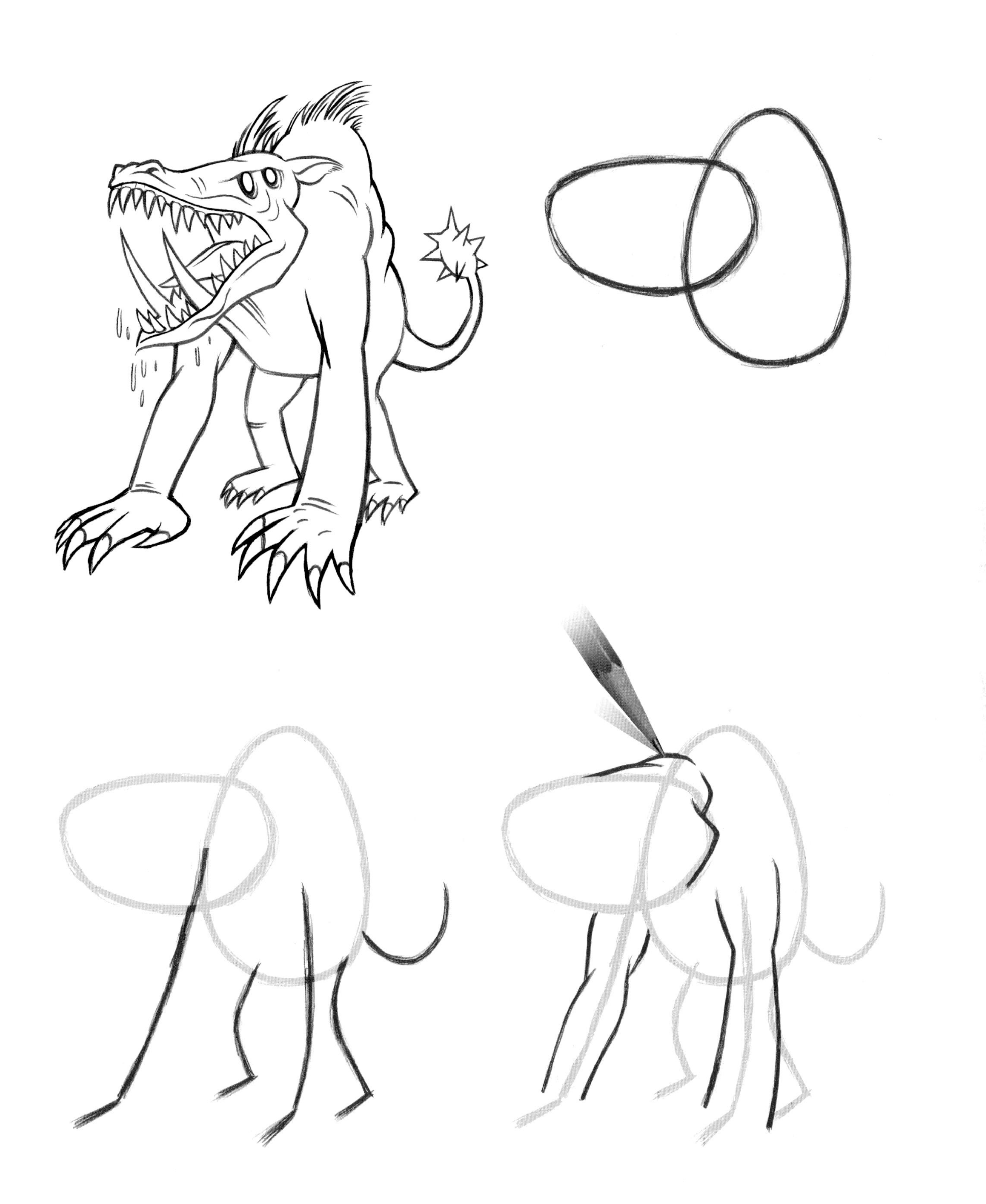

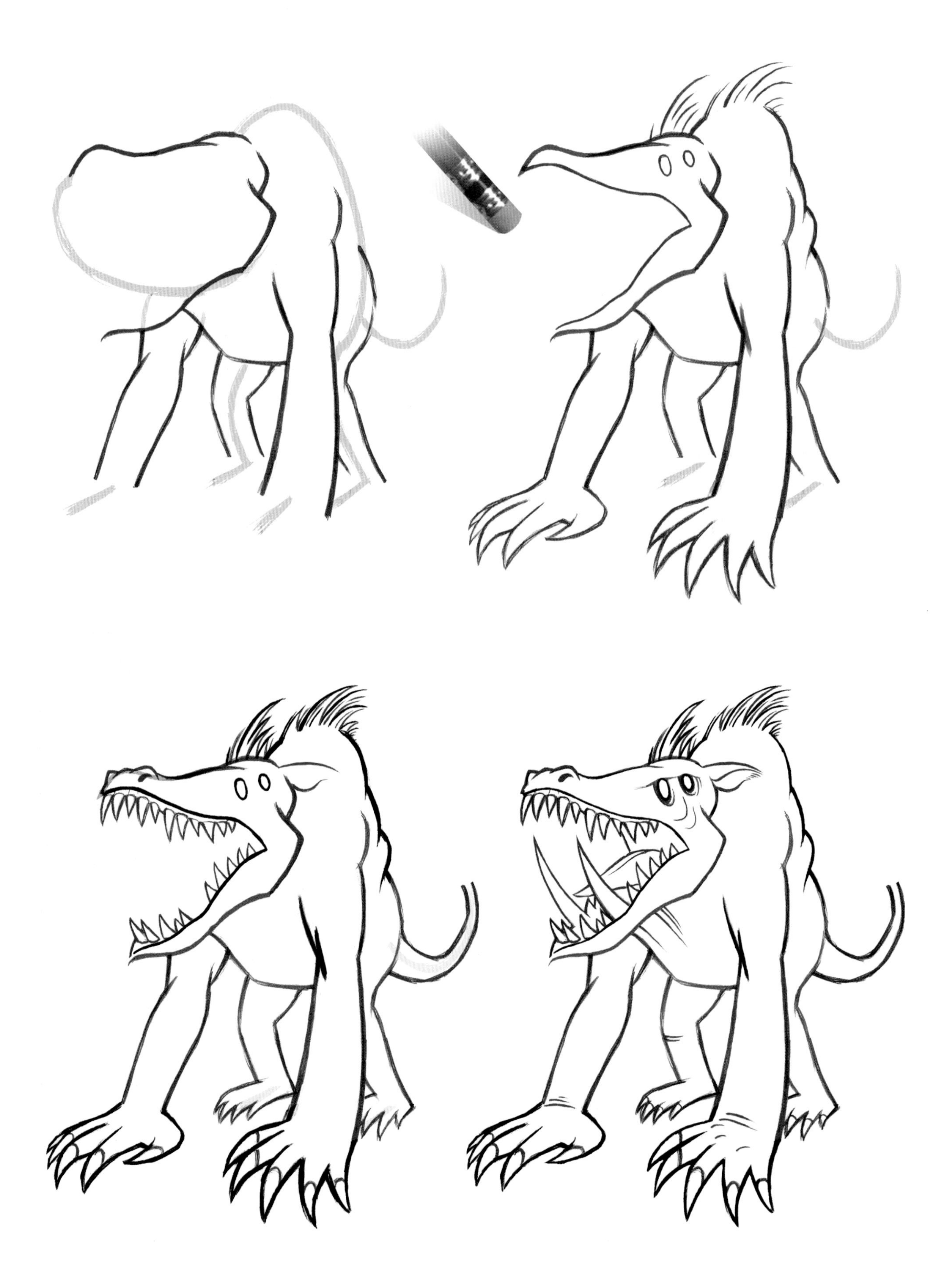

PERSPECTIVE IS ALWAYS USED WITH BIG BUILDINGS AND SUCH, BUT IT ALSO WORKS WELL WITH CHARACTERS.
I'M 4 FEET TALL...
NOW I'M 400 FEET TALL!

ZORT! HELP MEEE!!
HMM, I KNEW THIS BOOK WOULD COME IN HANDY ONE DAY...
ALL ABOUT SPACE DEVILS
SAYS HERE THE SABER TOOTHED SPACE DEVIL WILL ONLY EAT LIVE PREY...
QUICK, DEKE PLAY DEAD!
SNIFF SNIFF
WELL WHAT DO YOU KNOW? IT'S WORKING!
REALLY?
CHOMP!
GAAA!

OH MY GOSH, DEKE! THIS IS TERRIBLE! IT'S ALL MY FAULT! HOW COULD I HAVE BEEN SO...
BLEEP! BLEEP! BLEEP!
HELLO?
ZORT, GET ME OUTTA HERE!
DEKE! THANK GOODNESS YOU'RE ALIVE! SIT TIGHT, I'M ON IT!
EXCUSE ME SIR, OFFICIAL BUSINESS. WE'RE GOING TO NEED YOUR HOT DOG.
YOINK!
NOW TO EXCHANGE YE OLD FOOT-LONG, WITH YE OLD HIGH EXPLOSIVES...
HEY UGLY, HERE'S SOME DESSERT FOR YA!

OOOH! FOOT-LONG!
PLOP!
DON'T EAT THAT DEKE! JUST FIND YOURSELF SOME COVER.
THIS GUY'S ABOUT TO HAVE BIG-TIME INDIGESTION!
AND IT'S GOING TO GET MESSY!
KA-BOOM!
CONGRATULATIONS! YOU'VE JUST BLOWN UP YOUR ONLY GLADIATOR!
OH NO, DEKE! WHAT HAVE I DONE?
UH OH, HERE COME THE GUTS!
PLOOP!
SPLAT
PLOP!

Ye Pro Shoppe

A ROCKET BLAST OF FIRE IN THE PALM OF YOUR HAND! A REAL CROWD PLEASER.

"DEADLY ELEGANCE"... THAT'S WHAT YOUR OPPONENT WILL SAY AS HE IS CUT TO RIBBONS. THIS HAND-CRAFTED SWORD IS OVER 10,000 YEARS OLD. CUTS THROUGH ANYTHING, GUARANTEED!

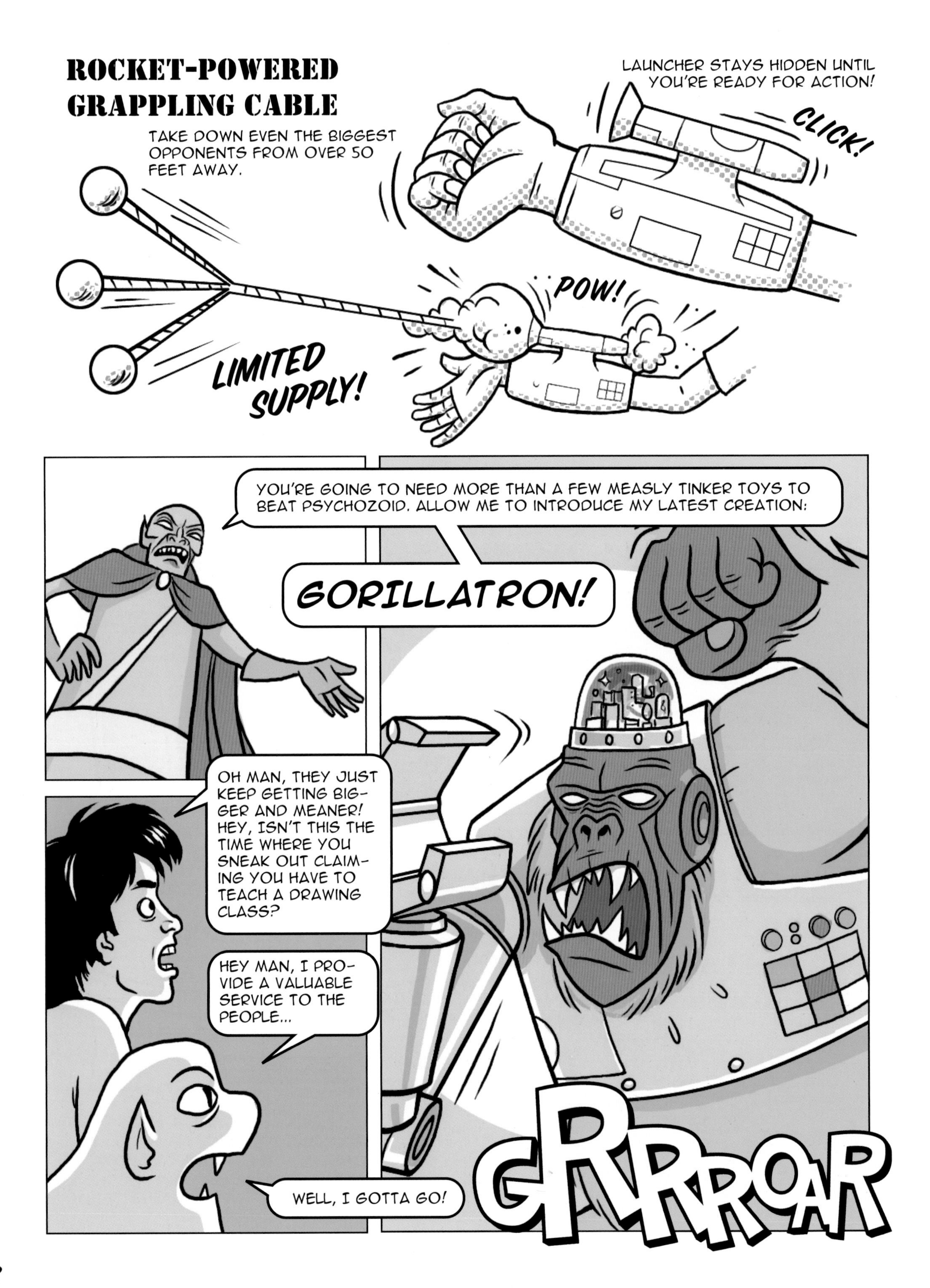
ROCKET-POWERED GRAPPLING CABLE
TAKE DOWN EVEN THE BIGGEST OPPONENTS FROM OVER 50 FEET AWAY.
LAUNCHER STAYS HIDDEN UNTIL YOU'RE READY FOR ACTION!
CLICK!
POW!
LIMITED SUPPLY!
YOU'RE GOING TO NEED MORE THAN A FEW MEASLY TINKER TOYS TO BEAT PSYCHOZOID. ALLOW ME TO INTRODUCE MY LATEST CREATION:
GORILLATRON!
OH MAN, THEY JUST KEEP GETTING BIGGER AND MEANER! HEY, ISN'T THIS THE TIME WHERE YOU SNEAK OUT CLAIMING YOU HAVE TO TEACH A DRAWING CLASS?
HEY MAN, I PROVIDE A VALUABLE SERVICE TO THE PEOPLE...
WELL, I GOTTA GO!
GRRROAR

Gorillatron

HALF BEAST, HALF MACHINE, THE GORILLATRON IS A SCIENCE EXPERIMENT GONE HORRIBLY WRONG. IN AN ATTEMPT TO CREATE THE MOST ADVANCED CYBORG WARRIOR, PSYCHOZOID SKIMPED ON SOME VITAL COMPONENTS AND THE RESULT WAS THIS 6,000-POUND NIGHTMARE! THE GORILLATRON IS A POTENT KILLING MACHINE, BUT HIS POSITRONIC BRAIN IS CROSS-WIRED AND FULL OF BUGS. YOU MUST OUTSMART THIS MONSTER BECAUSE YOU WILL NEVER OVERPOWER IT.

I'VE GOT TO GET ME SOME DISTANCE FROM THIS GUY, PRONTO!
CLICK!
THERE'S NO TELLING WHAT HE'S GOT UP HIS SLEEVE!
SSHOOOOM!
ROCKETS!
IF I TIME IT JUST RIGHT, THEN...
JUMP!
KA-BLAM

GORILLATRON, DO TRY AND AVOID KILLING THE AUDIENCE, I DON'T NEED ANYMORE LAWSUITS.
YOU'RE GOOD WITH THE GADGETS MONKEY BOY...
BUT HAVE YOU GOT THE SKILLS TO PAY THE BILLS?
NOW THAT'S A POSE! LET'S GET THIS ON PAPER BEFORE IT'S CLOBBERIN' TIME!

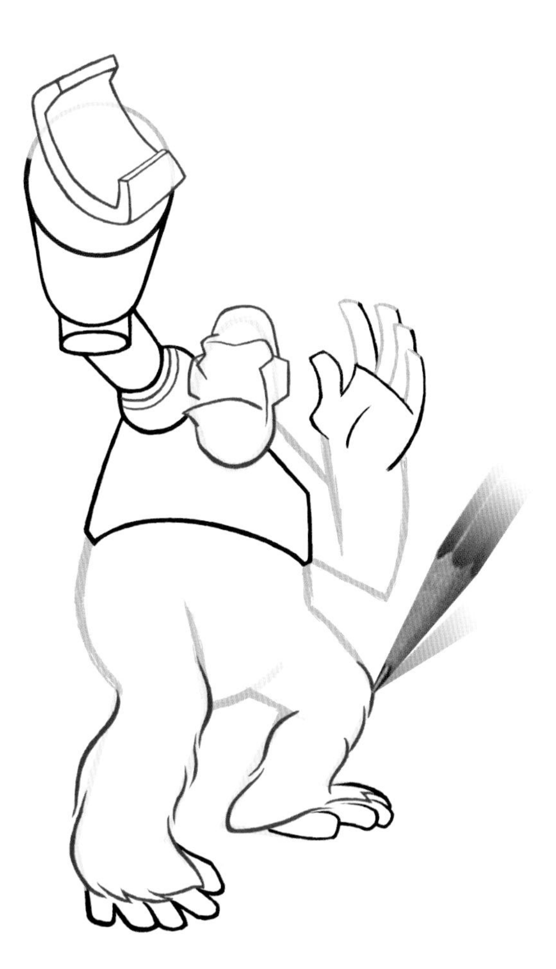

DRAWING FUR IS EASY. LONG HAIR USUALLY STARTS IN ONE SPOT AND HANGS DOWN, FOLLOWING THE CONTOUR OF THE BODY. FLUFFY FUR CAN START ANYWHERE AND TAKES ON A SHAPE OF IT'S OWN.

DEKE STARTS OUT WITH A ROUND-HOUSE KICK TO THE RIGHT...
BLOCK
...THEN ANOTHER KICK TO THE LEFT.
BLOCK!
THWACK!
GORILLATRON RESPONDS WITH A MASSIVE KICK TO THE CHEST.

OKAY, YOUR SKILLS ARE PRETTY GOOD. NOW IT'S MY TURN TO USE SOME GADGETS!
ROCKET-POWERED GRAPPLING CABLE!
NOW TO SWEEP YOU OFF YOUR FEET...
LIKE SO!
WHUMP
TIME TO LET THE SAMURAI 3000 FINISH THE JOB.

ALTHOUGH DEKE HAS NEVER WIELDED A SWORD BEFORE, THE SKILLS OF ANCIENT SAMURAI SEEM TO FLOW FROM THE MAGICAL WEAPON...
ATTACK!
WOW DEKE! YOU'RE JUST FULL OF SURPRISES! TIME TO DON OUR ARTIST CAPS AND CAPTURE THE ACTION!

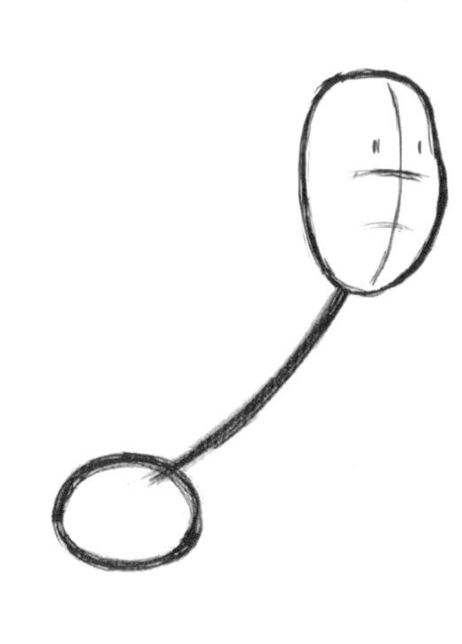

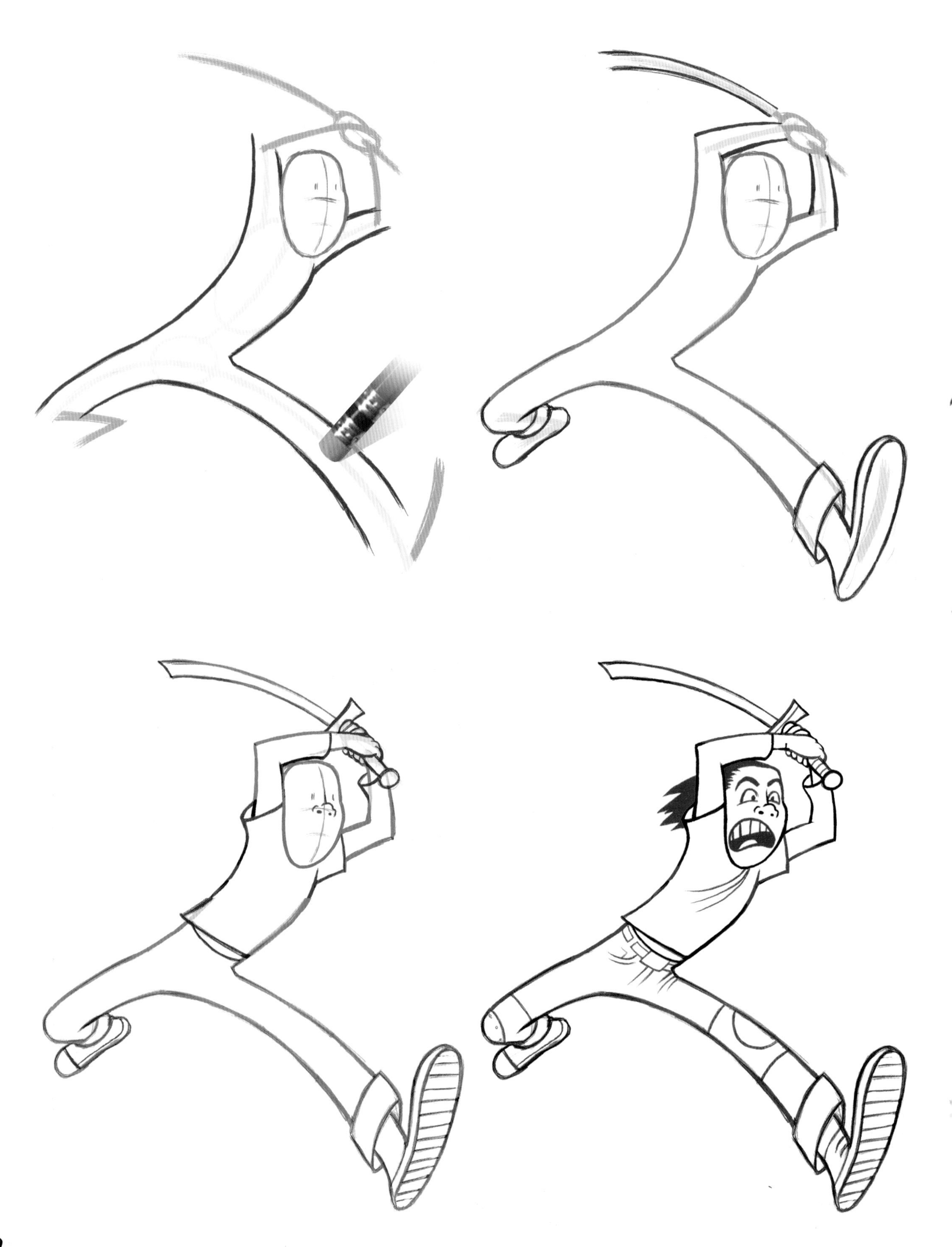

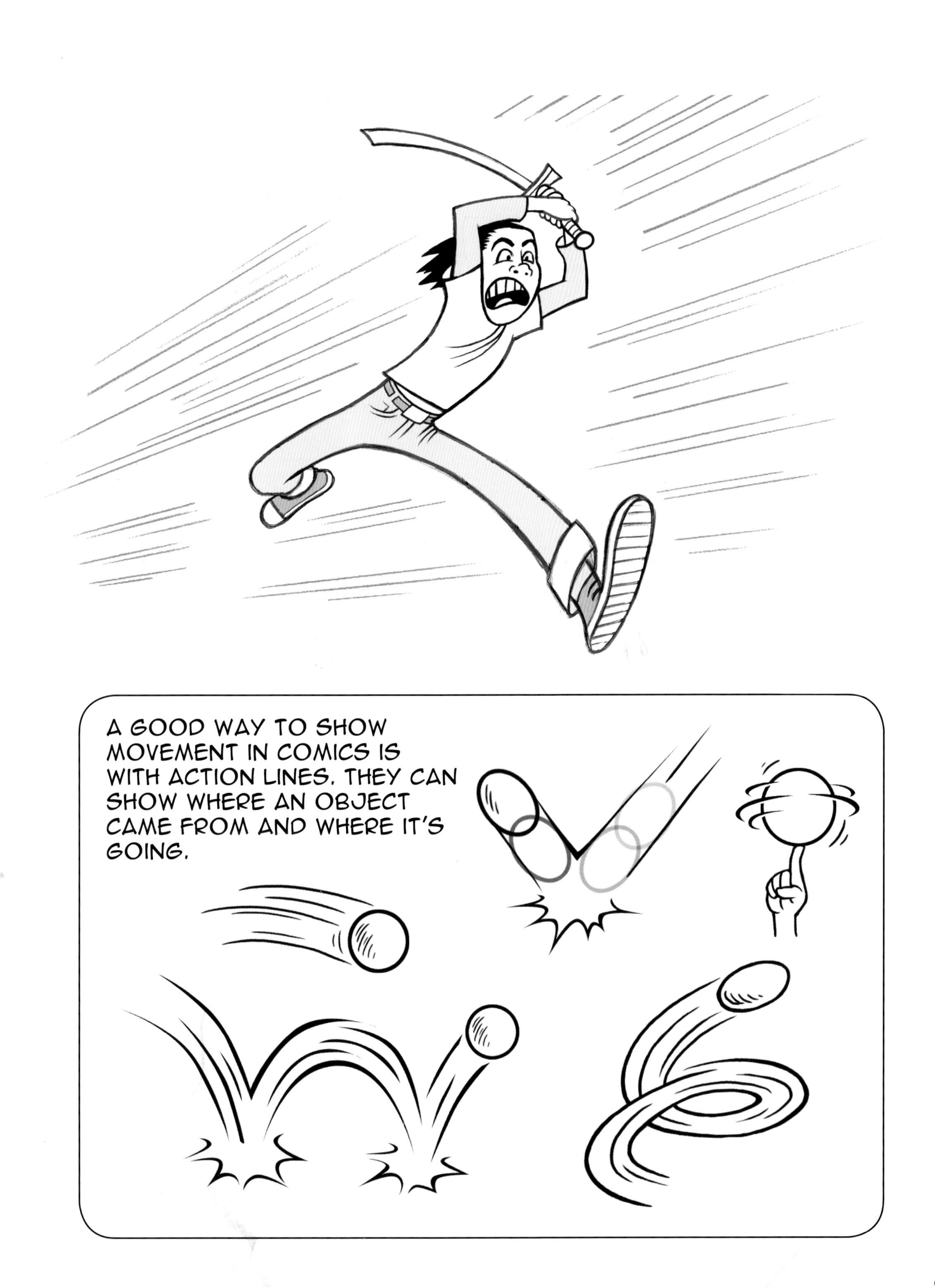
A GOOD WAY TO SHOW MOVEMENT IN COMICS IS WITH ACTION LINES. THEY CAN SHOW WHERE AN OBJECT CAME FROM AND WHERE IT'S GOING.

GORILLATRON LOSES AN ARM...
TANG!
...ONLY TO GAIN A SWORD!
SHING!
OH MAN,
I THINK I LIKED YOU BETTER THE OTHER WAY!
CLANG!
PLANG!
KANG!

THE TWO LOCK SWORDS FOR WHAT SEEMS AN ETERNITY.
TOO... POWERFUL... CAN'T... HOLD ON...
WHOOSH!
THUNK!
IT'S NOT THAT I'M NARROW MINDED...
I JUST BELIEVE ROBOTS AND GORILLAS SHOULD NOT CO-MINGLE.

CHOP!
CLUNK!
BZZZT!
BRAVO! ZORT, YOUR LITTLE HUMANOID IS DOING VERY WELL! PLEASE HELP YOUR-SELF TO ANOTHER SPREE AT OUR PRO SHOP!
CLAP!
CLAP!
CLAP!

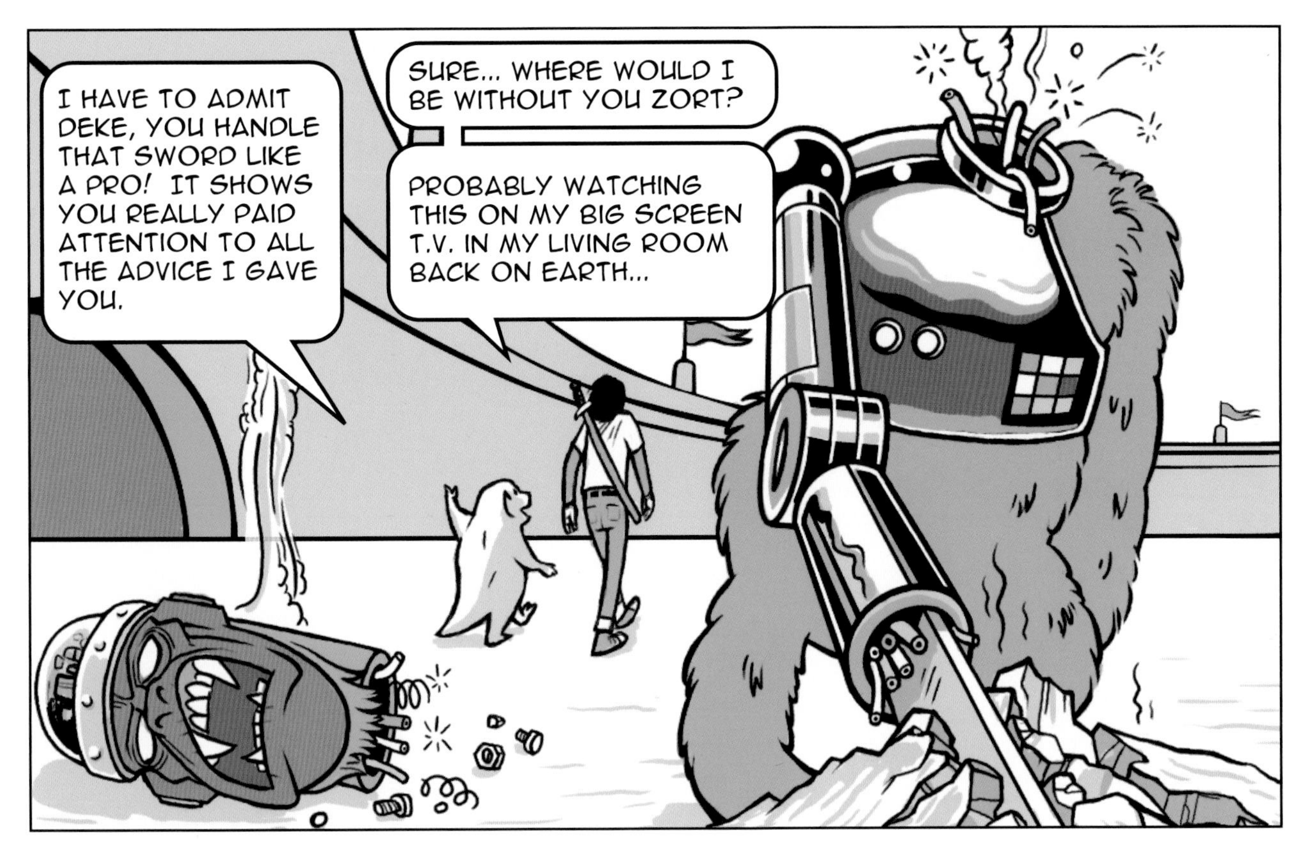

Ye Pro Shoppe

FREEZE GRENADE

Gift Pack!

HAND-HELD BALLISTIC DEVICE WILL ENCASE ENTIRE PERIMETER IN SOLID ICE!

SPECIAL

PERSONAL JET PACK

STRANDED ON A LIFELESS PLANET FOR ETERNITY? NOT TO WORRY; MAKE THE JUMP TO HYPER-SPACE WITH THIS LIGHT-WEIGHT PERSONAL PROPULSION UNIT!

1 MEGATON MINI-NUKE

WHY FUSS WITH A 'DIRTY BOMB' WHEN YOU CAN HAVE THE REAL THING?

NEW!

FORCE FIELD 'IN A RING'

VOICE-ACTIVATED MAGNOTRONIC SHIELD PROVIDES HIGH LEVEL OF PROTECTION IN A HANDSOME RING. OUR BEST SELLER!

WOW LOOK AT ALL THIS LOOT!
IF YOU THINK THIS IS OVER, YOU'RE SADLY MISTAKEN.
BRING OUT THE BEAST!
BEHOLD, THE LIVING NIGHTMARE OF ALL GLADIATORS...
TROG!

WOW! I HAVEN'T SEEN A TROGLOBRUTE IN YEARS. HANG ON A SECOND DEKE, I HAVE TO SHOW THE FOLKS AT HOME HOW TO DRAW THIS.
TAKE YOUR TIME!

Troglobrute

THE TROGLOBRUTE, OR 'TROG,' IS MORE CAPTIVE SLAVE THAN GLADIATOR. HIS DISMAL LIFE IS SPENT TORMENTED AND TAUNTED UNTIL ITS RAGE REACHES EXPLOSIVE LEVELS. IT'S THEN RELEASED INTO THE ARENA WITH A VIOLENT FURY FEW OPPONENTS LIVE TO TELL ABOUT. THE TROG'S EXTERIOR IS MADE OF SOLID ROCK, AND ALTHOUGH IT HAS NO EYES, IT USES GAMMA RAYS TO DETECT ITS OPPONENT.

COMIC ARTISTS OFTEN USE 'NON-PHOTO BLUE' PENCIL FOR ROUGH SKETCHES. IT DISAPPEARS WHEN PHOTOCOPIED.

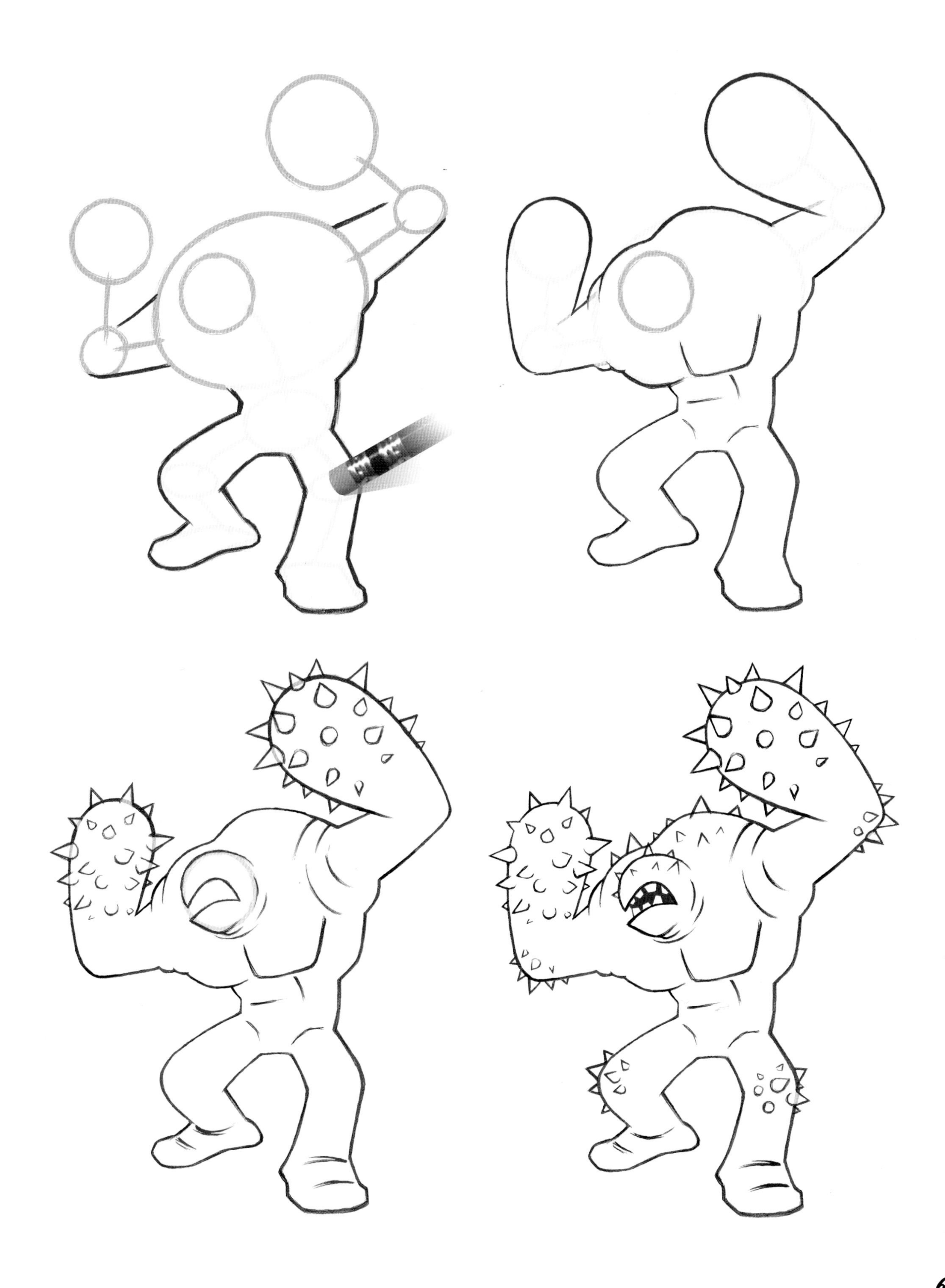

UNLIKE MOVIES, COMICS NEED WORDS TO SHOW SOUND EFFECTS. YOU CAN GO ONE STEP FURTHER AND BRING THOSE WORDS TO LIFE. TRY TO VISUALIZE HOW THE SOUND WOULD LOOK AND DRAW THE SOUND ITSELF!
ZAP
SWISH
CRACK
BOOOM!
RATTLE
SPLAT

WHOA!
BOOM!
DEKE, GET YOURSELF TO HIGHER GROUND!
DANG, WHAT IS THAT THING? SOME KIND OF CREATURE MADE OF SOLID ROCK!
I'VE SEEN SOME STRANGE ALIENS, BUT THIS ONE IS CREEPIEST BY FAR!
LET'S JUST HOPE HE CAN'T SCALE WALLS!

HEY, STONE FACE! WHY ARE YOU WORKING FOR THE PSYCHOZOID?
WHATEVER HE'S PAYING YOU IT ISN'T ENOUGH! I MEAN, THE WAY HE HAS YOU TIED UP LIKE THAT... IT'S JUST DEGRADING! YOU NEED TO FIND SOME REAL REPRESENTATION!
KRAK
GULP OR MAYBE THINGS ARE JUST FINE THE WAY THEY ARE!
YA KNOW WHAT YOU NEED?

A GOOD KICK IN THE PANTS!
BONK!
HA!
HA!
HA!
HA!
HA!
THANK YOU, THANK YOU VERY MUCH!
PSST! DEKE, BEHIND YOU!
POW!

WHAT THE??
THIS GUY REALLY WANTS A PIECE OF ME!
THWACK!

WHAT'S HAPPENING? LET ME SEE! LET ME SEE!
HANDS OFF THE ROYALTY!
SMACK!
THEY CONTINUE TO EXCHANGE BLOWS, ALMOST UNAWARE HOW FAST THEY ARE PLUMMETING TOWARD THE GROUND.

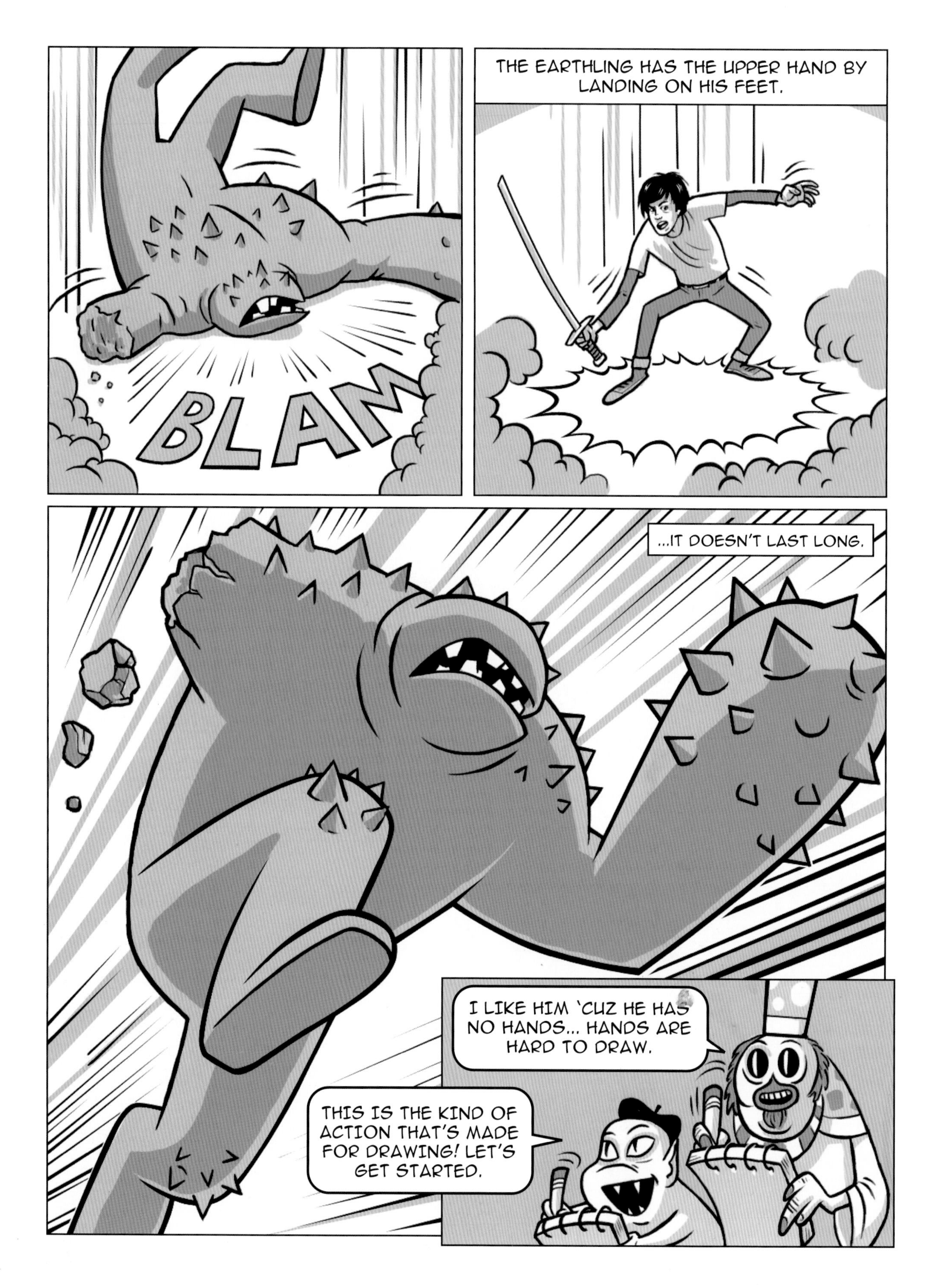
BLAM
THE EARTHLING HAS THE UPPER HAND BY LANDING ON HIS FEET.
...IT DOESN'T LAST LONG.
I LIKE HIM 'CUZ HE HAS NO HANDS... HANDS ARE HARD TO DRAW.
THIS IS THE KIND OF ACTION THAT'S MADE FOR DRAWING! LET'S GET STARTED.

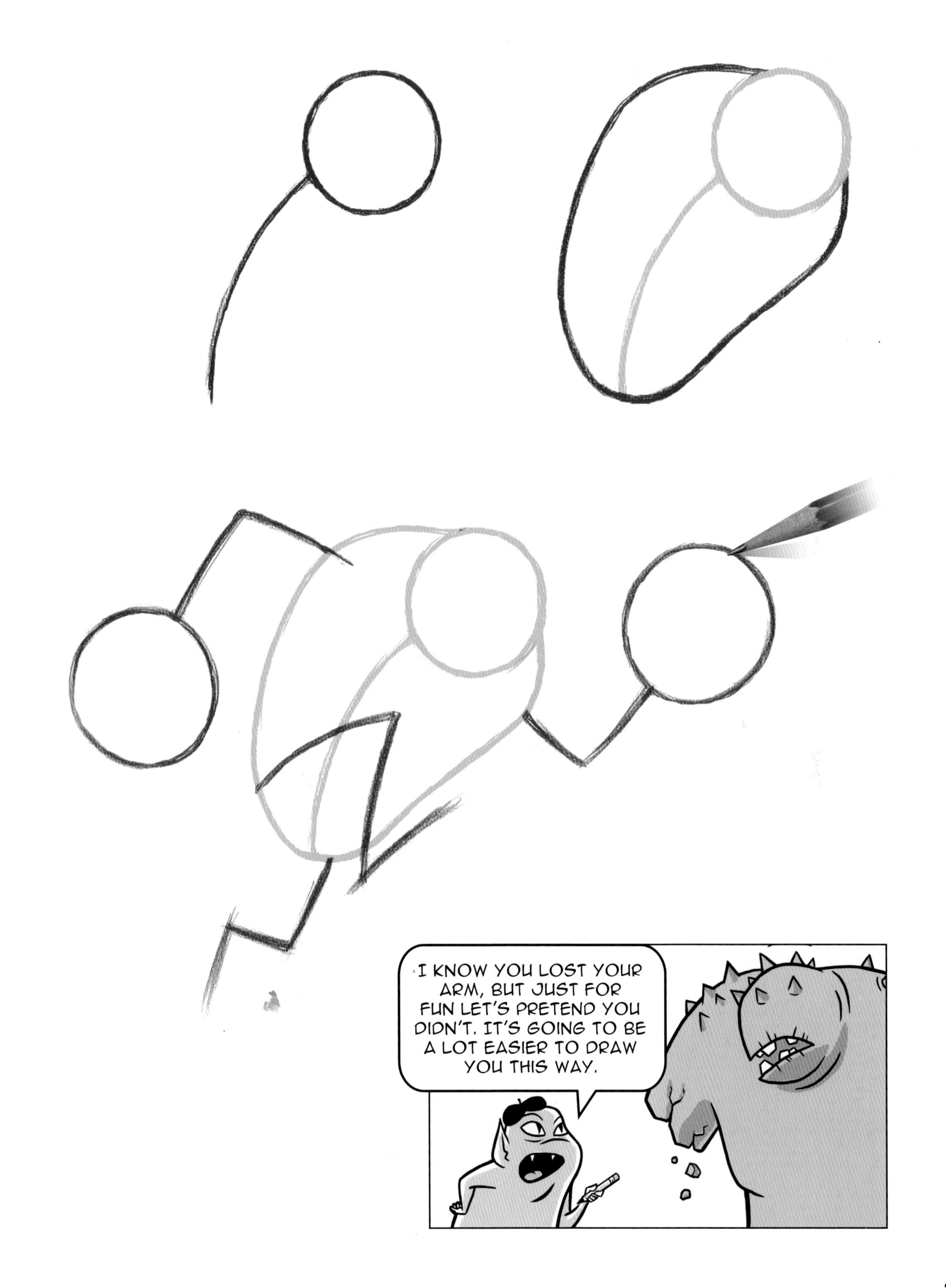
I KNOW YOU LOST YOUR ARM, BUT JUST FOR FUN LET'S PRETEND YOU DIDN'T. IT'S GOING TO BE A LOT EASIER TO DRAW YOU THIS WAY.

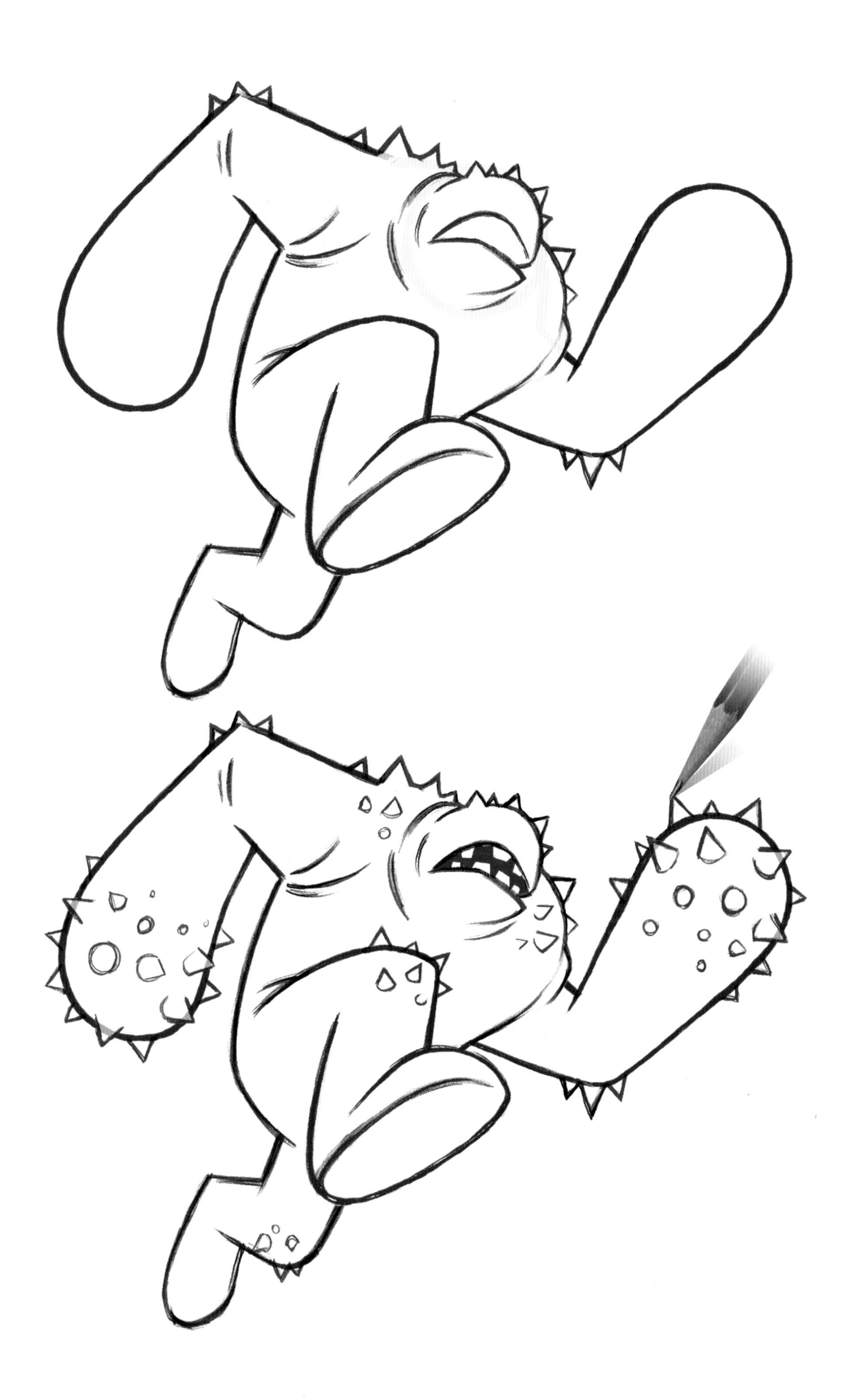

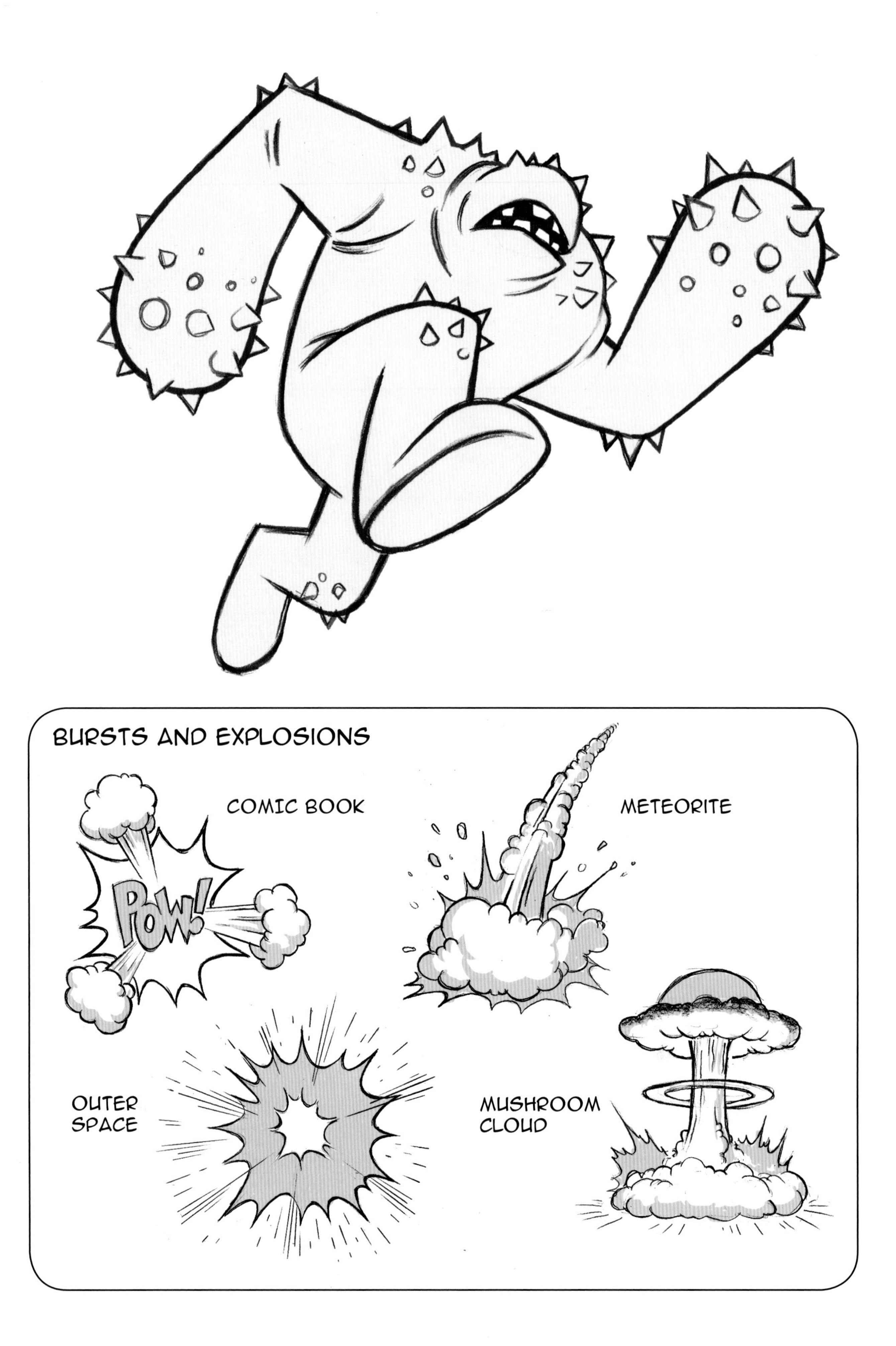
BURSTS AND EXPLOSIONS
COMIC BOOK
POW!
METEORITE
OUTER SPACE
MUSHROOM CLOUD

DON'T BE NERVOUS NOW. REMEMBER, YOU ONLY GET ONE SHOT AT THIS, DON'T SCREW IT UP...
OH YOU'RE BACK! ARE YOU SURE YOU DON'T HAVE TO TEACH ANOTHER DRAWING CLASS?
STEADY... STEADY...
NOW!!
AAAARG!

WHUMP!
NO! MY PRECIOUS TROG, WHAT HAVE THEY DONE TO YOU?
YOU! DO YOU KNOW HOW MUCH THIS GLADIATOR COST ME? YOU WILL PAY FOR THIS YOU INSOLENT HUMANOID!!
BRING OUT... THE LIL' CUTIE.
HELP!
LIL' CUTIE IS COMING!
RUN FOR YOUR LIVES!
OH, NO! NOT THIS THING AGAIN! GET ME OUT OF HERE QUICK!

ARE YOU SERIOUS? A GLADIATOR NAMED 'LIL' CUTIE'?
BOOM!
BOOM!
SAVE YOURSELVES!!
BOOM!
BOOM!
BOOM!
SMASH!
AWWW, LOOK. HE REALLY IS A LITTLE CUTIE! WHY HELLO THERE, LITTLE FELLA!

WHY THIS LITTLE GUY'S CUTE AS A BUTTON! I JUST WUV YOU, YES I DO! I WUV YOU!
UH DEKE, I WOULDN'T GET TOO CLOSE TO THAT THING...
NONSENSE, LOOK AT THOSE EYES. HE WOULDN'T HURT A FLY.
AWW, WHAT'S THE MATTER LITTLE FELLA? YOU GOT A LITTLE TUMMY ACHE OR SOMETHING? YOU LOOK KINDA FUNNY...
HULP!
HOLY SMOKES!!
IT'S MORPHING INTO SOME HUMONGOUS CREATURE!!

BEHOLD: DIABOLICUS ...OR, AS THE LOCALS CALL IT, 'LIL' CUTIE'
OKAY, OKAY. THIS ISN'T SO BAD. DO WE HAVE TO TIME TO DRAW THIS THING BEFORE IT EATS YOU?
CHOKE
MAKE IT QUICK!

Diabolicus
(or Lil' Cutie)

NO ONE IS SURE OF ITS ORIGINS, BUT IF THERE IS A PLACE CALLED HELL, DIABOLICUS LIVES THERE. THIS NIGHTMARE DRAWS ITS VICTIMS CLOSE BY PRETENDING TO BE AN ADORABLE LITTLE CUTIE PIE. ONCE IN RANGE, THE CREATURE REVEALS ITS DEADLINESS. EACH OF ITS THREE HEADS MUST BE SEVERED BEFORE THE BEAST WILL DIE. (AND YOU WILL NEVER LOOK AT A BABY KITTEN THE SAME WAY AGAIN!)

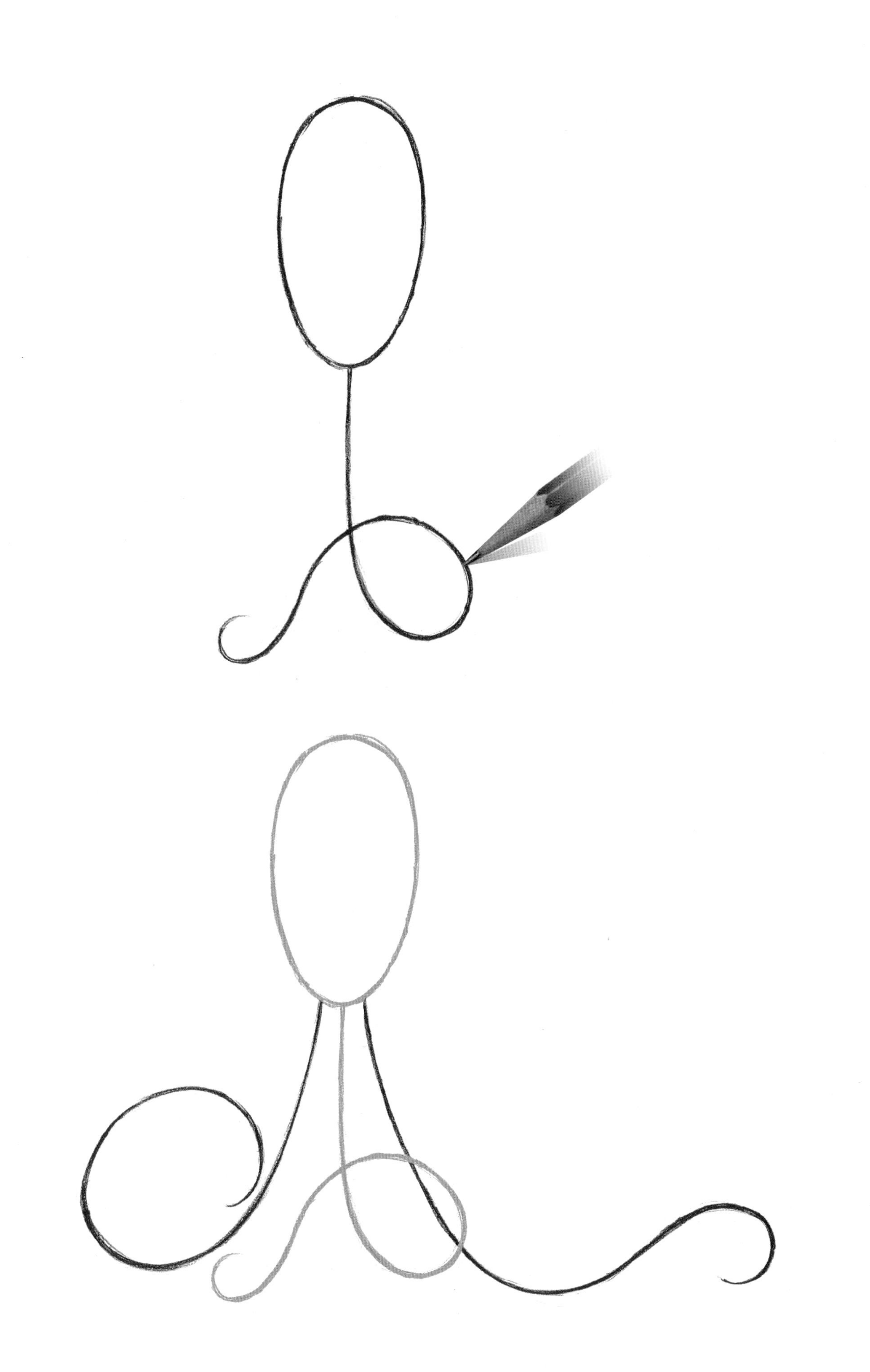

DEKE TRIES HIS BEST NOT TO SHOW HOW SCARED HE IS AS HE MANAGES TO GET ONE ARM FREE.
OH, YOU WANT A PIECE OF ME?
NOT TODAY, FISH FACE!
PUNCH!
CHOMP!
AAAAARGG! MY FIRST WORK-RELATED INJURY!
MUST... THINK OF... SOMETHING... QUICKLY!
WAIT, I ALMOST FORGOT...
MINI FLAME-THROWER!

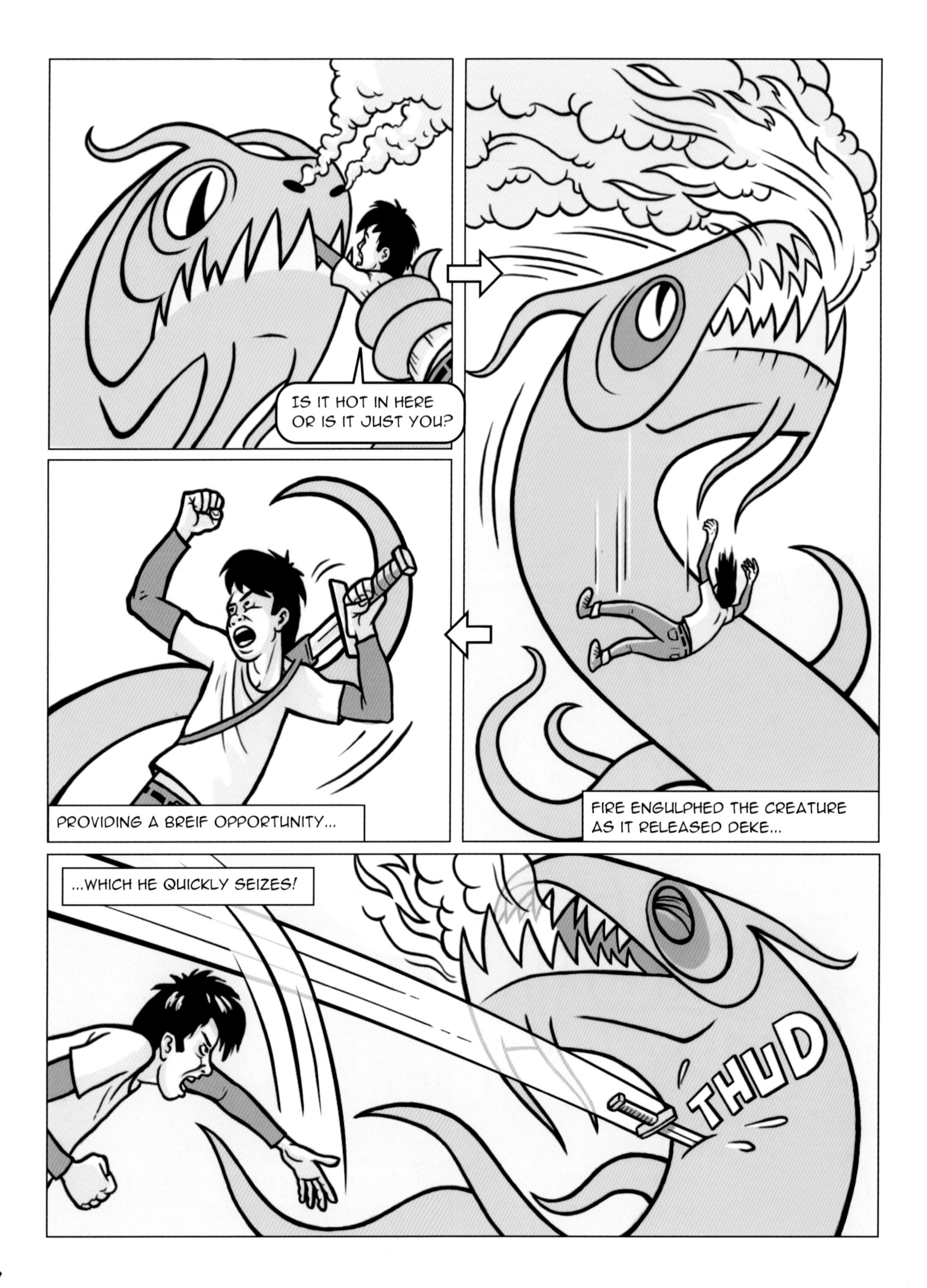
IS IT HOT IN HERE
OR IS IT JUST YOU?
FIRE ENGULPHED THE CREATURE
AS IT RELEASED DEKE...
PROVIDING A BREIF OPPORTUNITY...
...WHICH HE QUICKLY SEIZES!
THUD

MINUTES LATER...
THAT WAS WAY TOO CLOSE ZORT!
YOU'RE DOING GREAT OUT THERE. HE'S AFRAID, WHICH MEANS YOU'VE GOT THE UPPER HAND NOW...
GOSH, DO YOU REALLY THINK SOOOOOOOO!!!
WOOSH!
I DEMAND A REMATCH. THIS IS NOT A FAIR FIGHT!
JAB!
CHOP!
FIRST THING I'VE GOT TO DO IS GET BACK ON TWO FEET...

BEFORE DEKE COULD REGAIN HIS FOOTING, HE FOUND HIMSELF TRAPPED ONCE AGAIN!
DON'T LET HIM STING YOU, DEKE!
YEAH, THANKS FOR THE ADVICE, ZORT.
I REMEMBER WE HAD A GIANT BUG PROBLEM BACK HOME...
POKE!
WE JUST STOMPED THEM DEAD.
THIS ANCIENT SWORD TOOK CARE OF BUSINESS BEFORE...
LET'S HOPE IT WORKS AGAIN!

TWO DOWN...
ONE TO GO!
THWAK!
OH WOW, YOU REALLY MADE HIM MAD. THAT WAS HIS FAVORITE MONSTER-HEAD-TENTACLE THING.
YEAH, THIS HAS BEEN THE TOUGH-EST FIGHT SO FAR AND IT'S NOT OVER YET. I'VE GOT TO FIND A WAY TO OUT-SMART THE MAIN HEAD.
OKAY, WHILE YOU'RE DOING THAT I'M GOING TO SHOW THE FOLKS AT HOME HOW TO DRAW THIS THING.
DON'T DIE UNTIL I GET BACK.

UH-OH! QUICK, COMPACT SHIELD!
TANG!
PING!
PING!
IF I STAND STILL, I DIE!
BAM
WAY TO KICK HIM IN THE EYE DEKE!
I TAUGHT HIM THAT ONE!

NASTY BIT OF BUSINESS THIS THING IS...
HUH? IT'S GOT MY LEG...
CHOP
AS LONG AS MY BLADE STAYS SHARP, I CAN CHOP MY WAY THROUGH THIS GUY.
WHOA! THIS IS MORE THAN I BARGAINED FOR.
IT JUST KEEPS COMING AT ME FROM EVERY DIRECTION!
TOO MANY TENTACLES... THEY'RE OVER POWERING ME!
THIS CAN'T BE THE END... THERE'S A BUNCH MORE PAGES LEFT!
CAN'T... BREATHE... GASP LOSING... CONSCIOUSNESS....

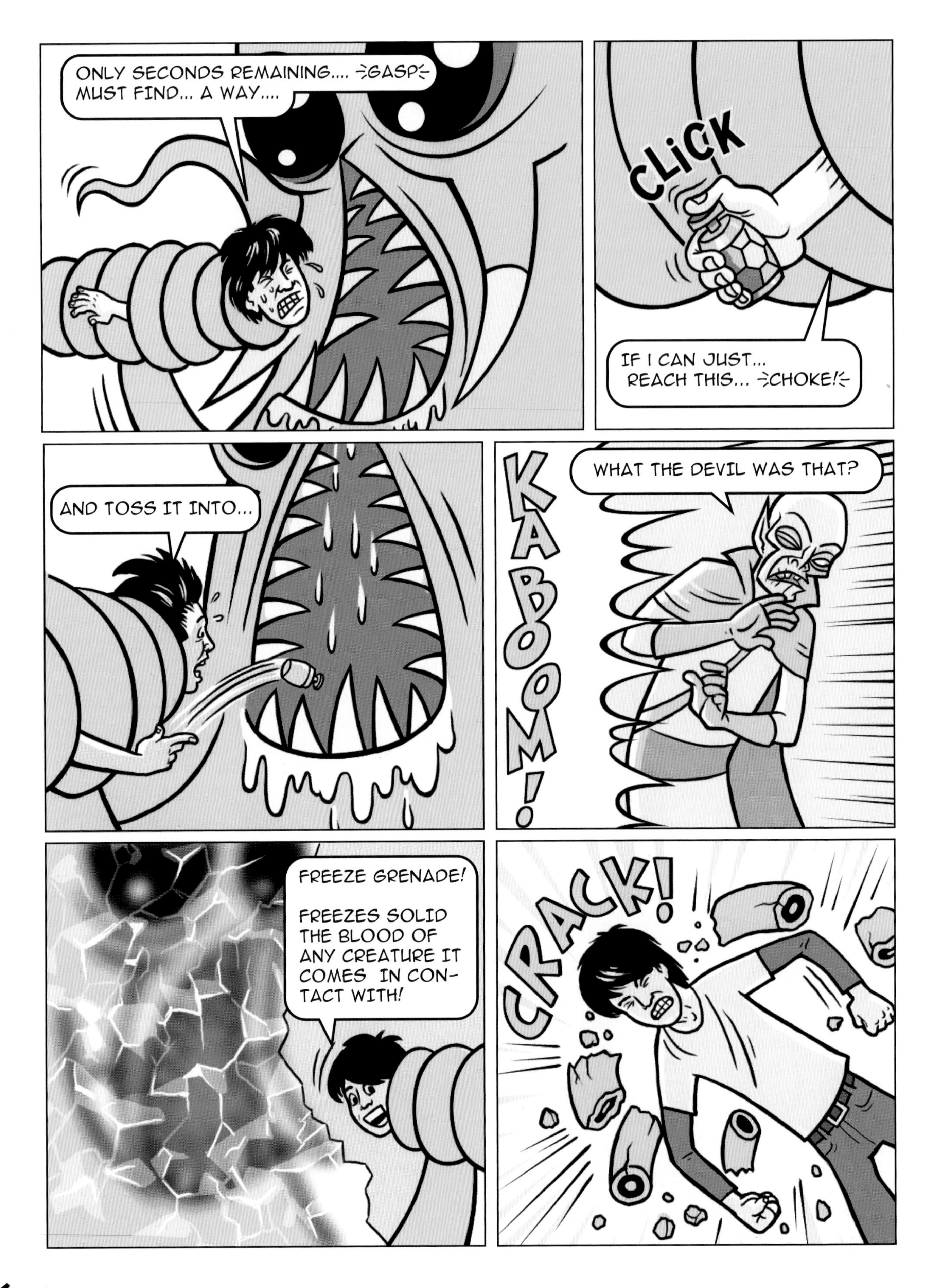
ONLY SECONDS REMAINING.... ⪾GASP⪽
MUST FIND... A WAY....
CLICK
IF I CAN JUST... REACH THIS... ⪾CHOKE!⪽
AND TOSS IT INTO...
KABOOM!
WHAT THE DEVIL WAS THAT?
FREEZE GRENADE!
FREEZES SOLID THE BLOOD OF ANY CREATURE IT COMES IN CON-TACT WITH!
CRACK!

CRACKLE!
MONEY WELL SPENT, I'D SAY!
CRUMBLE!
NO, THIS CAN'T BE! IT'S IMPOSSIBLE!
'FRAID SO PSYCHO, LOOKS LIKE I WIN THE CHAMPIONSHIP AFTER ALL! DON'T WORRY, THERE'S ALWAYS NEXT YEAR, OR THE YEAR AFTER THAT...
YOU INSOLENT REPTILE, YOU HAVE FOILED MY PLANS FOR THE LAST TIME!
AWW, DON'T BE THAT WAY OLD PAL! I CAN PROBABLY FIND YOU A JOB SOMEWHERE CLEANING OUT GLADIATOR CAGES!
I summon the powers of darkness from all the corners of the universe!
MAN, TALK ABOUT A SORE LOSER! LET'S YOU AND ME HEAD OVER TO THE V.I.P. LOUNGE.
SURE... UH WHAT THE HECK IS THAT? WHERE DID PSYCHOZOID GO?

THE PSYCHOZOID WILL NOT BE DEFEATED! I WILL DESTROY YOU MYSELF THIS TIME.
WHOA, CHECK OUT THE PSY-CHOZOID! HE'S SUPERSIZED... AND HE'S GOT AN ATTITUDE!
I WAS AFRAID THIS MIGHT HAPPEN. HE ALWAYS BRAGGED ABOUT SUPER POWERS, BUT WHO KNEW HE WAS TELLING THE TRUTH?
DEKE, GO GET A SMOOTHIE OR SOMETHING. PSYCHOZOID NEEDS TO HAVE HIS FACE REARRANGED.
BUT I'M GOING TO GIVE ONE LAST DRAWING LESSON BEFORE HE GETS THE SMACK DOWN.

The Psychozoid

HE WASN'T ALWAYS ZORT'S NEMESIS. AS A YOUNG MAN PSYCHOZOID WAS AN EXCEPTIONAL STUDENT WITH DREAMS OF USING HIS SUPER INTELLIGENCE TO MAKE THE UNIVERSE A BETTER PLACE. HOWEVER, HE WAS A NERD AND, AS SUCH, HE WAS SUBJECT TO RIDICULE BY PRETTY GIRLS AND REGULAR BEATINGS BY THE JOCKS. HIS ANGER TURNED TO RAGE AS HE VOWED REVENGE ON ALL LIVING THINGS. APART FROM BEING AN EVIL GENIUS, PSYCHOZOID POSSESSES BASIC WIZARDRY SKILLS SUCH AS LEVITATION, HYPNOSIS, AND THE ABILITY TO SHOOT ENERGY. AS YOU CAN SEE HERE, HE CAN ALSO CHANGE HIS SIZE DRAMATICALLY.

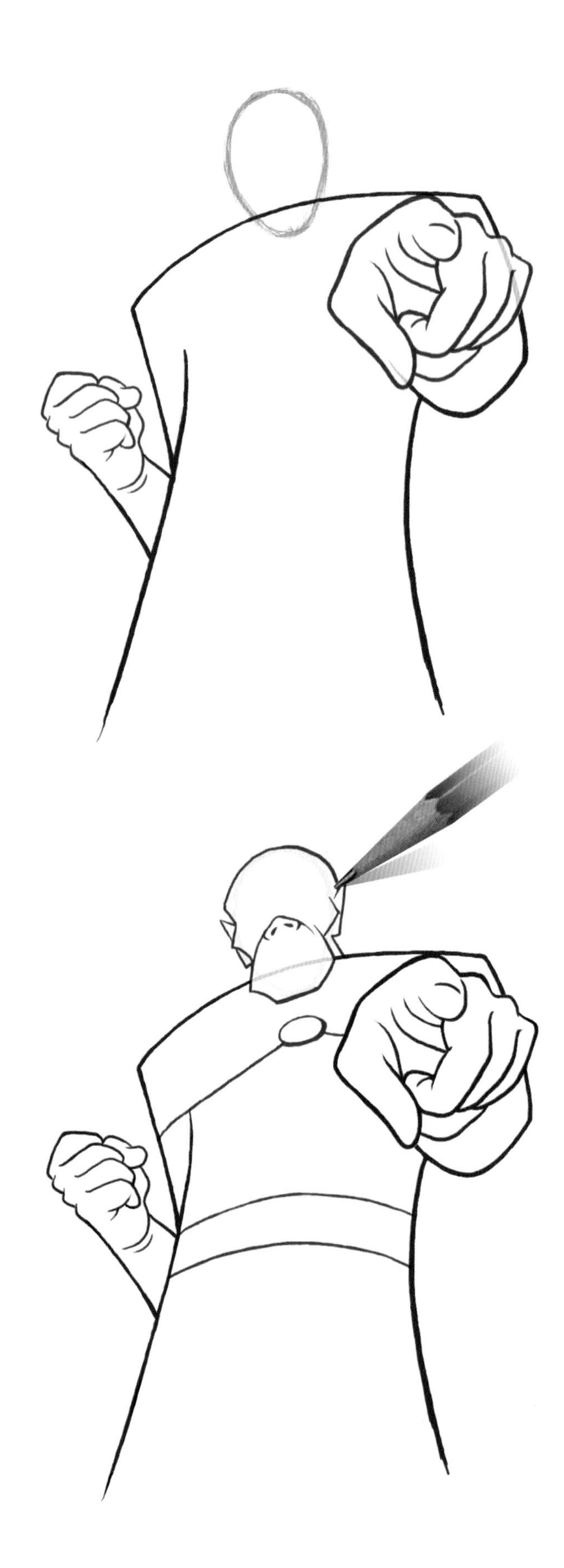

OH BOY, THIS IS GOING BE GREAT FOR THE RATINGS GUYS!
CLAP! CLAP! CLAP!
C'MON PSYCHOZOID, LET'S SEE WHAT YOU'VE GOT!
CAREFUL ZORT, HE'S USING SOME KIND OF MAGIC.
MAGIC? HA! YOU HAVEN'T SEEN ANYTHING YET!
TELL ME PSYCHOZOID, WHY DO YOU NEED TO GET SO BIG TO FIGHT A LITTLE GUY LIKE ME?
COULD IT BE YOU'RE NOT ABSOLUTELY CERTAIN YOU CAN WIN THIS TIME?
HA, YOU'VE BLABBED YOUR TRIVIAL BUNK FOR THE LAST TIME YOU PIDDLING, INSIGNIFICANT SIMPLETON.
BUNK HUH? LET'S JUST SUPPOSE FOR A SEC-OND THE UNTHINKABLE HAPPENS...

SUPPOSE I DEFY ALL ODDS AND ACTUALLY BEAT THE TAR OUT OF YOU?
POW!
FLIP!
AND I WIN THE SPACE MONSTER BATTLE PLANET CHAMPIONSHIP TITLE...
WHAK
...THE FAME, ...THE RESPECT, ...THE CHICKS!
...NOT TO MENTION ALL THAT MONEY THAT GOES ALONG WITH IT. NOW TELL ME, WHAT WOULD YOU DO IF THAT EVER HAPPENED?
I'LL SHOW YOU WHAT WOULD HAPPEN!
DEKE, THROW ME YOUR SWORD!

KLANG!
CANG!
KLANG!
KLANG!
KLANG!
KLANG!
TANG!
PANG!
OH CRAP!
HEH HEH, NOW LET'S NOT BE TOO HASTY THERE, OLD PAL. VIOLENCE NEVER SOLVED ANYTHING...
ANY LAST WORDS YOU'D LIKE TO SAY BEFORE I CAST YOU INTO OBLIVION, YOU PATHETIC FOOL?
UH YEAH, I HAVE A FEW...
HUH??

IF YOU PASS BY PLANET EARTH SAY HELLO TO MY MOM, WOULD YOU?
PERSONAL JET-PACK
YEAH, IT'S BEEN A REAL BLAST WORKING WITH YOU PSYCHOZOID!
MINI-NUKE
NO! NO! WHAT'S HAPPENING?
FWOOOOOOOOSHH
YOU HAVEN'T HEARD THE LAST OF MEEEEEEEEE
BOOM!
YOU HAVE A MOM?

THE END... SEE YOU NEXT SEASON!

HERE ARE SOME BONUS CHARACTER DESIGN SUGGESTIONS!

HEADS

The most important part about creating an alien creature is the face. It says everything about the personality. The eyes, nose, ears, and mouth can be anyplace or nowhere at all. Below are a few examples of very different creatures created with the same basic shapes.

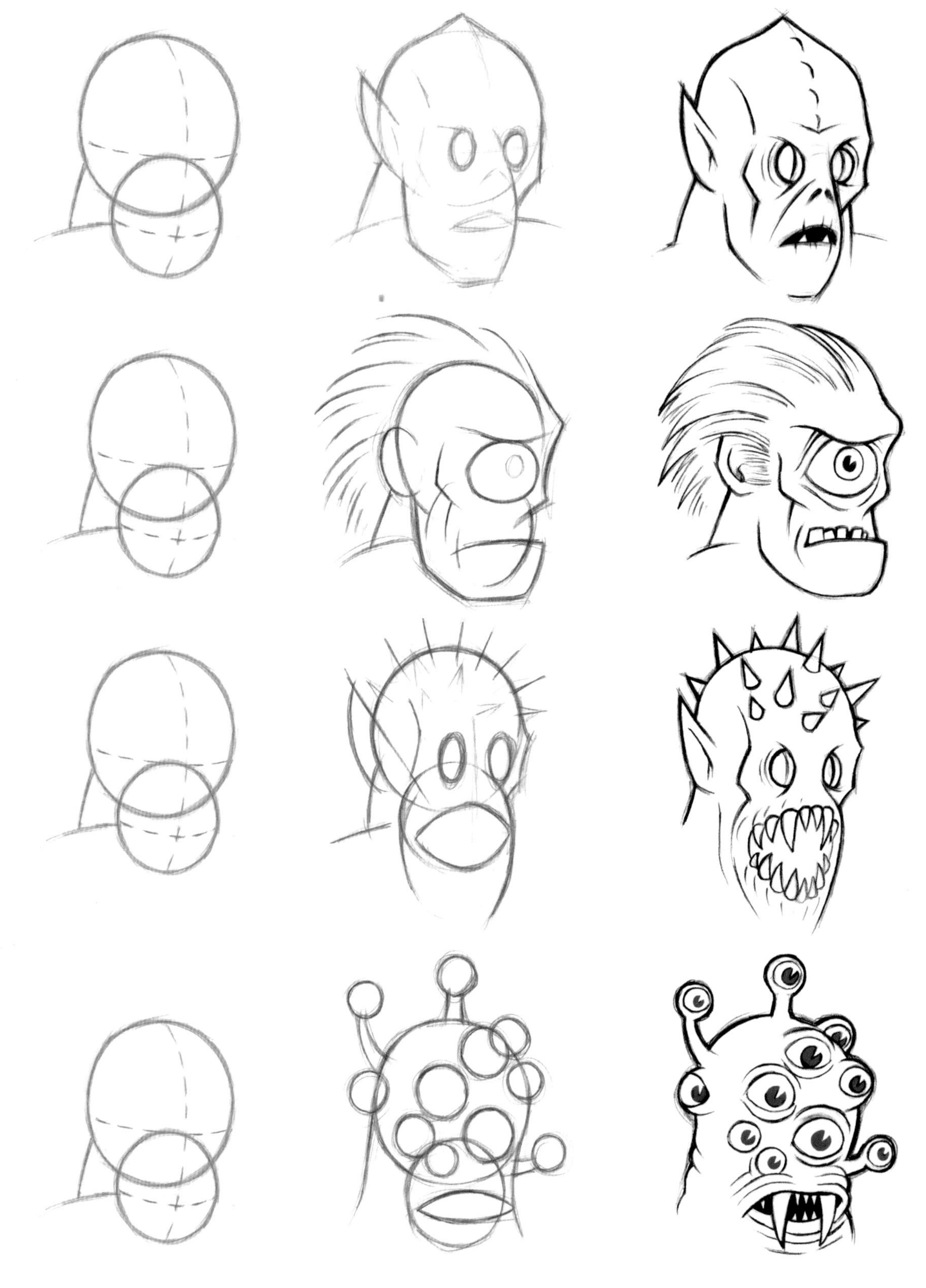

EYES

If you're going to draw eyes at all, the placement and size is important. Big bug eyes are good for brainy time travelers, whereas deep-set, hooded eyes depict more strength and dominance. Generally, most alien eyes are drawn without pupils. This makes the creature look more mysterious. Drawing the two eyes different sizes creates a more deformed or mutated alien.

Deep-set, hooded eyes create a sinister, mysterious look. Instead of pupils, try a solid color or glow.

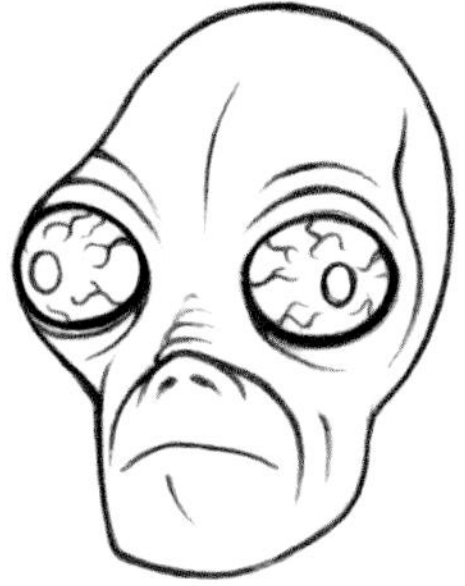

For crazier or insane look, try pushing the eyes outward, popping out of the head. Use veins to exaggerate.

Lowering the eyes to nose level makes your creature more amphibious, or frog-like. Try using vertical reptile pupils.

Placing very small eyes close together make for a dumb, or easily frustrated character.

NOSES

Most artists ignore the nose when designing aliens, or they make it very small. Be different—add a prominent snout on your beast.

Big creatures are more likely to have a big nose. Add some nose jewelry to give him the look of an ancient race.

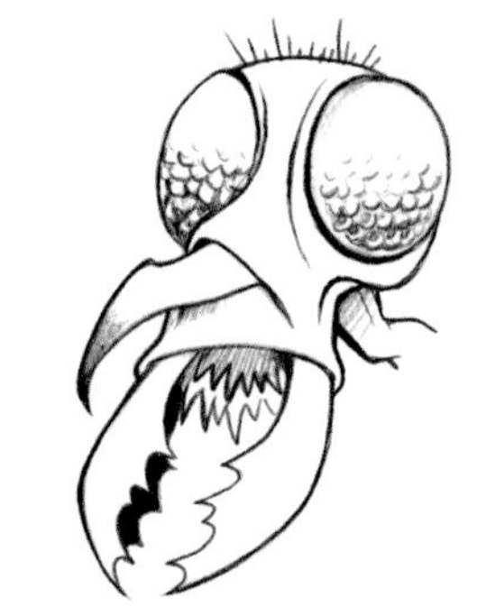

Insect aliens can have noses too. It's a good place to have a deadly stinger.

Don't be afraid to use animal noses on your aliens. This guy has the snout of a wild boar.

The head of a dino-reptilian character is almost all nose.

TEETH

I think you'll agree when I say nothing makes a character more threatening than a mouthful of razor-sharp teeth. Fangs and such can be a little tricky at first. It's helpful to examine the skull of an actual predator, such as an alligator or tiger.

When drawing fangs, it helps to study the skull of an actual predator.

Crooked and chipped teeth with an under bite can look menacing.

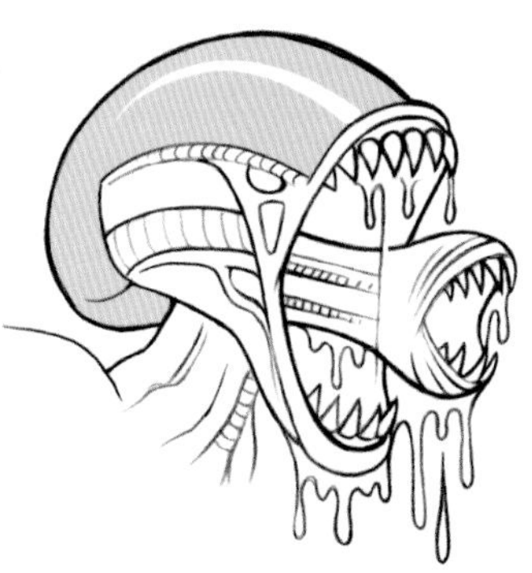

Popular Hollywood aliens sometimes have a mouth within a mouth.

HANDS

Not all aliens have hands. But if you want to create them, here are some helpful hints: Smarter, less physically threatening creatures have long, skinny hands, which are more useful for operating computers and laser guns than for hand-to-hand combat. Two or three fingers are all he needs.

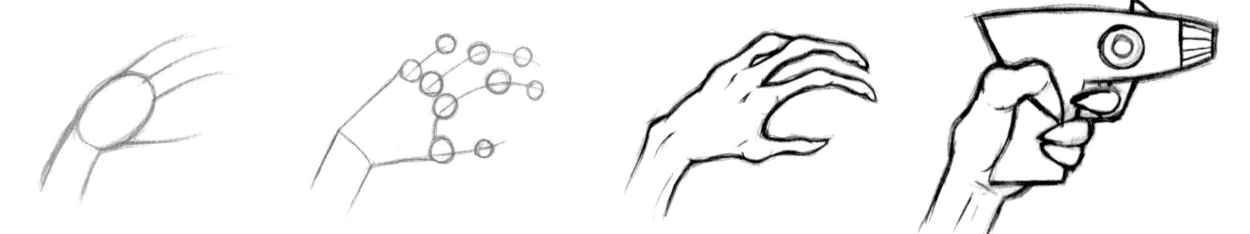

The giant hands of an alien warrior usually need good, sharp claws to help grab their victims. Sometimes they wear battle gear such as spiked leather wrist bands. The fingers are short and thick.

Robots can change out their hands.

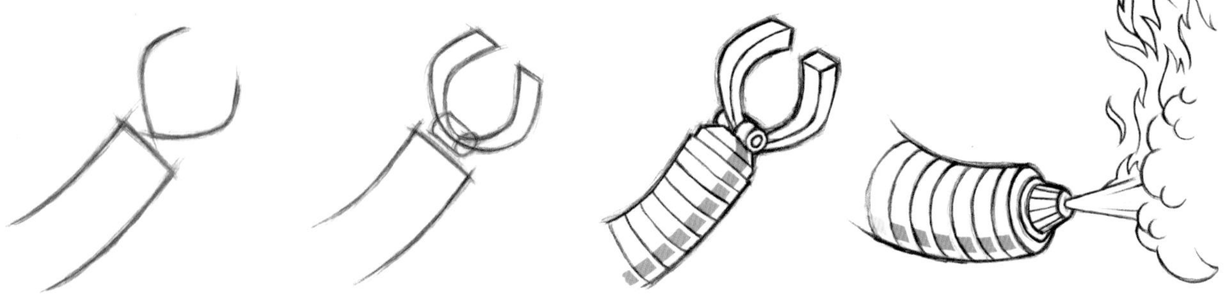

FEET

The feet are just as powerful as hands, but they're more vulnerable. Make sure you add some defensive armor.

Most do not wear shoes, but if they do, it's usually some kind of armored space boot with concealed weaponry or rocket boosters.

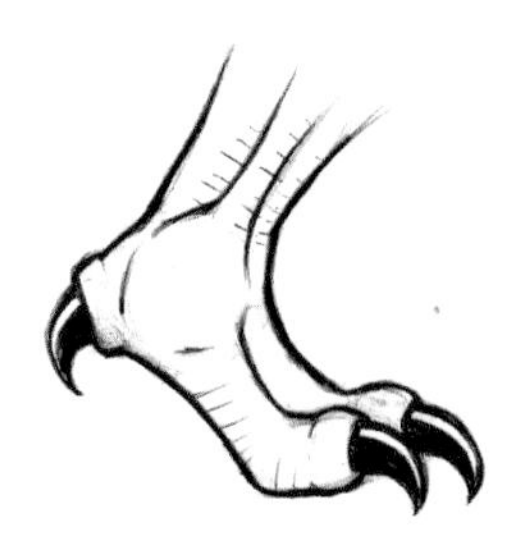

In the wastelands of distant planets, aliens need good, strong feet. Warriors need large claws for fighting. Many times, dinosaur feet work well.

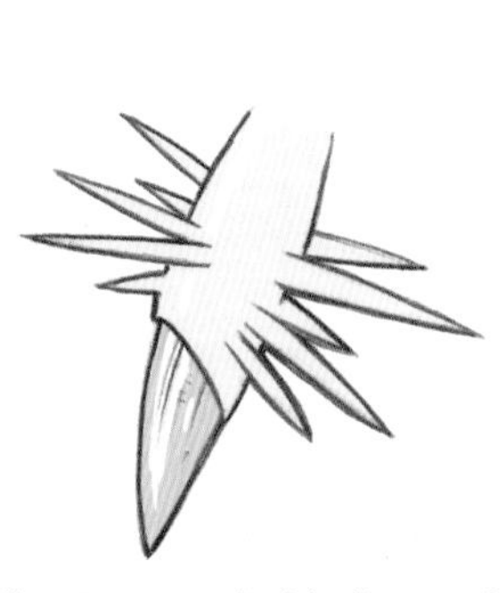

Planets covered with slime and goo are where you can find creatures with high-traction spikes. Leave the ends open if you want them to shoot poison rockets.

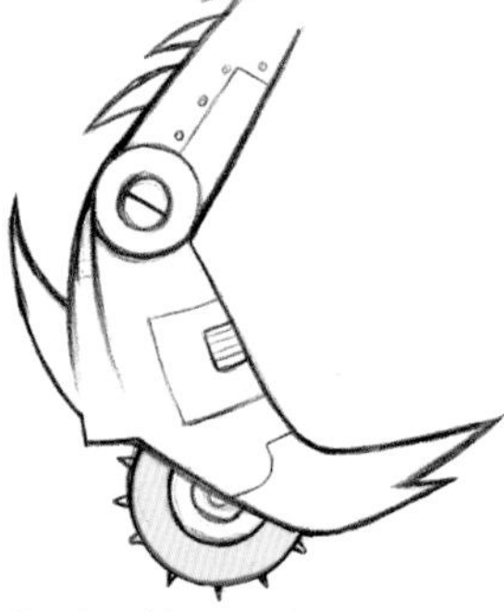

If a droid loses a leg, it can easily be defeated. They need special armor to stay mobile. If wheels are used, they need to be concealed.

SETTING UP YOUR SCENE

When setting up your scene in a drawing or comic, you're doing the same job as any famous movie director. It's important that your audience sees exactly what you want them to see, in the best way possible. Try to imagine that you are viewing the comic book panel through the lens of a camera. You can tilt, zoom, pan... actually you can do much more than any camera can! The position of the camera has a huge impact on the feeling of the scene. Just watch any action movie on T.V. and notice how they change the camera angle to alter the mood of the story. The illustration below shows how one scene can have a completely different feel just by changing camera angles.

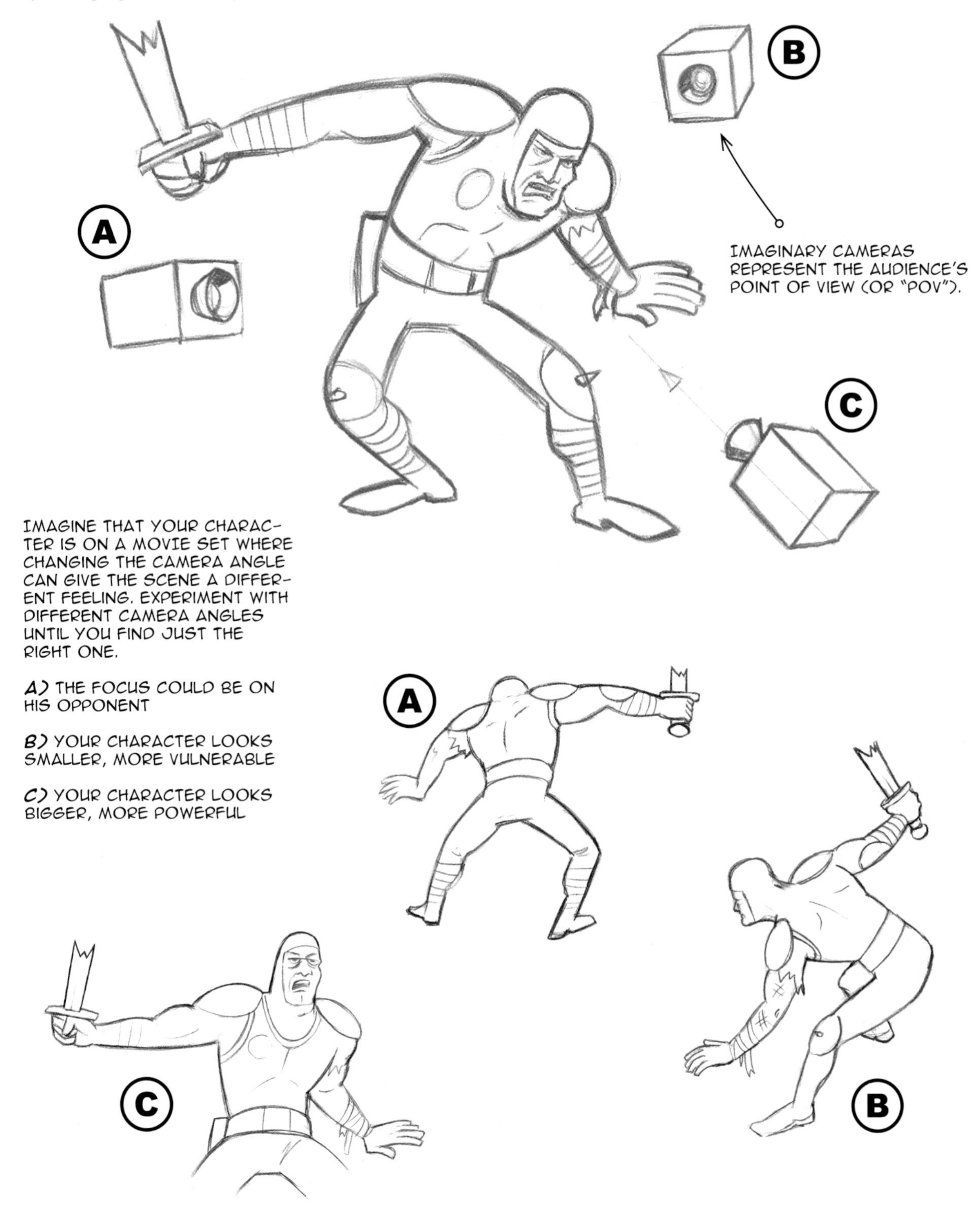

ABOUT THE AUTHOR

During daylight hours, **Dana Muise** is an animator working in the broadcast and T.V. cartoon industry. By night he lives in the world of comics, monsters, and space creatures. When other kids were learning how to draw happy trees and rainbows, he was perfecting his army of giant claw creatures as they prepared to battle the menacing space bugs on Planet Zoltor. The only thing he likes better than space monsters is teaching people how to draw them. As far as he knows, space monsters are real and we should know how to draw them before they get here. Dana attended Massachusetts College of Art in Boston and the School of Visual Arts in New York. He lives in beautiful San Francisco, California, with his talented artist wife Leigh and daughter Eva, who is his favorite little monster of all. Below are some of the many drawings he made as a kid. Dana notes, "I especially thank my dad for holding onto these as I grew up!"

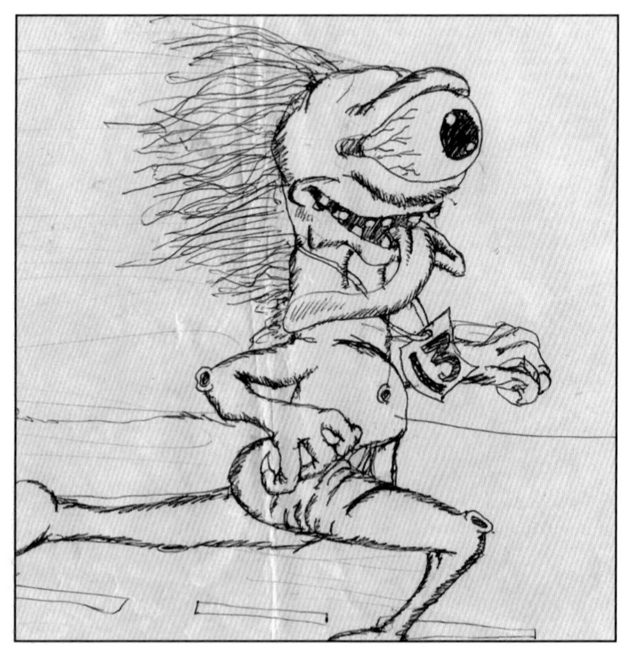

Monster On The Loose! Dana Muise: Age 7

Space Trooper Under Attack Dana Muise: Age 8

War on the Planet Xelton Dana Muise: Age 9

Super Awesome Space Battle Dana Muise: Age 10